Labor to Leadership
My Journey from Pit Digger to CEO

Jeremy Torisk

Dedication

In honor of your service and in thanks for your friendship. I dedicate this book to Lt. Col. Frank Damiano 10/3/1944 - 11/22/2020 United States Air Force (ret). Bronze Star recipient, Vietnam.

Contents

Acknowledgements

I'd bet that everyone has a pie in the sky goal that could be called a "someday goal." For me, one of those has always been to be a published author.

I was always told, "You need to tell people about these stories. You have a book in you!" And I would always reply with, "Yeah, one day, one day."

Well, today is that day! I know me, and for me to do this, I needed to have a greater goal than just to put my stories on paper or on this Mac monitor, as it were. So, I got a greater goal.

I decided now that my kids are grown up for the most part, and they are bright enough to not make the mistakes I mention in this book, I can mix those stories with another passion I have recently developed.

There has never been such ease in reaching people through the internet, video conferencing, YouTube channels, podcasts, virtual teaching, etc. I want to use technology and dedicate this stage of my life to helping people who either want to start or have already started a small business but have no clue that there is so much more to running a business than just being the best at what you do in your industry. I want to help those who feel stuck in a corporate role get noticed and start climbing that ladder.

There are amazing employees who have so much more to offer the company or want to take the leap into entrepreneurship and put the control in their own hands. Also, there are countless part-time solo acts, like real estate agents, plumbers, landscapers, etc., who are working a full-time job while trying to make enough at their side hustle to quit the J.O.B. (Just Over Broke).

Unfortunately, most do not know the broad spectrum of knowledge they will need to gain and master to make the dream work.

Through years of trial and error (mostly error), I have adopted the systems and processes it takes to succeed, and I want to share these experiences so these people will know what they are in for and can be prepared to make the commitments needed to have a shot at hitting their business and personal goals.

America is truly a wonderful place for motivated employees and small business owners, because the very foundation that America was built on was a do-over. People from all over the world have come here to begin a new life, where their efforts can be rewarded. And just because you may have been born here does not mean you will not fail. It doesn't mean you weren't born into a world of shit with circumstances uncontrolled by you. Or that you won't take a while to get the "stinkin' thinkin'" out of your system, to quote the great Zig Ziglar. It means that even though you may have had all of those events or worse happen in your life, you still get a second chance…and a third chance…and a fourth…and a fifth. You get the point. However, it is important not to forget these mistakes, to forgive yourself for making them, to learn from them, and, just as important, not to repeat them again and again.

Most people are afraid of taking a chance because they may fail. I argue that they will fail, and I encourage failure at all levels of your life! The only way you can guarantee that failure will not happen is if you fail to start anything. And then you have failed at living. FAIL = First Attempt in Learning. To quote my favorite football coach of all time, Don Shula, "It's the start that stops most people."

This book is dedicated to all the people in the many stages of my wild, crazy, amazing, and sometimes unbelievable life who make it possible for me to act on this calling.

So, to name names:

To the many mentors, some of whom I know and have worked closely with and some of whom I follow on social media and read about in books, thank you for creating paths I could travel and for leaving the clues from your success. I have named them before, but here is as good a place as any to bore people:

Nestor Martin – Nestor had the largest impact on my professional and personal life. He was one of the first who offered me real career and life guidance, although he admitted later that he actually voted against me for a position at the time. I am still trying to live up to your standards! Thank you, Nestor.

Michael Aronowitz – A man with so much talent, a man I was so intimidated by, but who challenged me and eventually rewarded me by restoring the diminished confidence I had in myself. Thank you, Mike.

James Flynn – A man who showed me the power and the art of conversation. He truly takes real interest in everyone he sits with. A great lesson in selflessness. Thank you, James.

Wes Parsons – My brother from another mother, who is the king of relationship building. He made me come out of my shell and grow from discomfort to the man I am today who lives to connect! Thank you, Wes.

To those who helped and guided me through the writing process:

Michael Sabbag – Thank you for your advice and exemplary leadership.

Annie Leib –Thank you for helping me edit my book and sharing your *AnnieTude* every day!

The Nudelberg Huddle Gang – Thank you, Steve and Marc, for connecting me with the most amazing and supportive circle of caring professionals on the planet and inventing The Virtual Coffee!

To my family:

My dad, Rat – The man who is my father in every real sense of the word. The funniest man I have ever known. Even after an unimaginable loss. I love you, Pop.

My mom, Becky – That woman thinks I walk on water without getting my feet wet. A woman who has faced more than most could imagine living through and hasn't lost her capacity to love. Most don't understand her, but I do. Sometimes so much so that it scares me. I love you, Ma.

To my kids – in order of age, so no fighting!

Suzanna (Zanna), my dwata – I am so lucky…no, I am blessed…to have you in my life! Your fierce loyalty to this family will never go unappreciated. You have so much to look forward to, and I can't wait to take that journey with you! I love you, Zanna.

Trace(y), my first-born son – I will never forget the feeling of your first day on earth. Like me, you are a protector, helping people in their most vulnerable time. You aim to run into the burning buildings when everyone else runs out. You will realize that dream and much more. I love you, Tracey.

Garrett (Gar), my not-so-mini me – A gladiator who has an entrepreneur's heart and a blind eye to challenges. You see life as a huge pool of success, and you have jumped in with both feet and made a huge splash. With your thirst to learn and serve, you will help more people achieve success than I will ever get to. I love you, Gar.

Peter (Pete), my drumming protégé and the smartest kid of the bunch! – You will never know how much I admire the way you think and your big ol' heart! Your future is unknown right now, but that leaves so much to imagine. You will have all of my support no matter what you decide to do with your life. I love you, Pete.

To my sister Paulette and my nephews and nieces Anthony, Tosha, Chey, Lil Michael, Andy, Annie, Alex, Ava, and AJ. To my brother Wes. You are missed every day. To my beautiful Aunt Kathy and my Superman, Uncle Lew. To the greatest brother- and sister-in-law a husband could ever wish for (11-9-4-life)! To all my cousins and lifelong friends like Pat, John, Kim, Robin, Scirocco Bobby, Manny, Andy, Brice, and my hero, Tony. To my babies' mama, Laurel, and their amazing stepdad, Jodie, and to all the Hutchings women. Thank you. I truly love you all.

Saving the best for last, thanks to my best friend, partner, and beautiful wife:

Christy – Without her being a beacon of confidence, love, and trust, I would surely be lost.

Living with me is tough under the best of circumstances, but living with me through a pandemic lockdown, a crazed mission to write a book like this, along with running the businesses and keeping the 9 to 5 going is a lot to ask of anyone.

Thank you for your patience, cooperation, and for listening to me record every episode of my podcast 52 times each in the beginning! I love you more than you will ever realize.

Finally, to all of you who thought you had me pegged from day one, thanks for the fuel.

Introduction

Do you have a position in a company you like? Do you enjoy great health insurance coverage, two weeks' paid vacation each year, a 401(k) match, all on the company's dime?

There is only one problem. You have been in the same position for three years now, and it seems like your colleagues have all been promoted, and you cannot get one interview for an open management position.

Or maybe you are an *amazing* employee who can envision taking the leap and going out on your own so you can stop making the bosses rich and begin building your own legacy.

You have real ambition and are realizing every day that you punch a clock, and someone else is capitalizing from your time and skills. After all, is it really all that hard to run a business? Everyone tells you how this place would be nothing without you there doing all the heavy lifting!

I bet you can identify with these circumstances.

I have been through both of the above scenarios a few times, and in *Labor to Leadership* I share my personal journey from cable company pit digger to C-level executive and business owner with all the ups and downs in between.

I have created new businesses time and time again across different types of industries, and they all began with such gusto and hope! And they almost all ended with a whimper. Some lasted longer than others. I will not bore you with national statistics about how few new companies make it through their first year or sit here and make excuses for how many mistakes I made in my businesses. You have Google to look up those stats, and I don't make excuses…not anymore.

Not only will I share the keys to what is involved in mastering the skills it takes to climb a corporate ladder or begin and operate a successful business, but I will show you how critical your mindset is in determining your success or failure.

I know firsthand how important that is. I will share with you how as a "poor kid from the wrong side of the tracks" I had absolutely no clue that I would go on to help so many people and change so many lives…for the better.

There was a time in my life when I could never even have imagined I could rise through the ranks of a corporate American company or be in a position to teach anyone what it takes to start and run a new business successfully, because as a kid I grew up in an environment where I was surrounded by drugs, alcohol, all types of abuse, and daily street fights.

Back then, the game plan was simply not to die, or to stay out of jail, or not to give into all of the drugs and alcohol that were so prevalent in my life.

There was absolutely no such thing as ambition or a future. I lived in the moment until I was 20 years old.

That is when I experienced an event that changed the direction of my life forever in an instant.

As a result of one sentence on one phone call, I was released from my past. I didn't know it at the time, but I had experienced a total mindset shift. Because of this, I exploded in the workplace and transformed from someone who just had a job to executing a plan that allowed me to navigate my way from being a field laborer to climbing the ladder into middle management. Then, with that experience and some newfound confidence, I was brave enough to step outside the comfort and security of that corporate American behemoth to start running businesses of my own!

I am a serial entrepreneur! Yes, my last name is spelled TO-RISK, and my blood type is B-POSITIVE! How could I possibly fail?

But I went years making mistakes that sunk any shot of having my efforts pay off, because the things that needed to happen every day to have long-term success were not being done!

After many attempts at making a go of it on my own, I eventually got wise. I swallowed my pride, set aside my (very large) ego, and accepted that there is little about managing people, clients, or a company I could invent on my own that hadn't been written about and taught already.

I certainly couldn't achieve success without ever knowing what real success looked like. I finally understood that I just had to follow the blueprints of those who came before me and did what I want to do!

So, I started investing in me! I went out and got a knowledge education! I attended numerous workshops, seminars, and conventions. I hired consultants, sought mentors, and read everything I could get my dyslexic mind to wrap around. I developed a givers mentality. It was no longer about me! Everything I did was to help others.

That is when I went from merely moving one step forward and stumbling two steps back to experiencing true success! Now, when I put my mind to something, I use the tools I have acquired, and I excel at it.

Over the last 30 years, I have worked with various company owners to build and maintain multimillion-dollar revenue streams in local, national, and international markets, and have had the honor to help rebuild the CATV and Telephone systems for many communities after multiple hurricanes over the years to include Puerto Rico, The Virgin Islands, The Bahamas , the Fl Keys and even my own home town in South Florida!

These are the results of making decisions to act at the speed of instruction, of owning a driven mindset to achieve and succeed at what I choose to pursue by feeling passion not for the results, but for the pursuit itself.

When 2020 presented so many challenges, including lockdowns, I tried to think of a way to take advantage of the downtime and began a new journey, one I always had on my bucket list but never thought there would be a reason for beyond reliving my life in my head and putting on paper for the cathartic value, acknowledging the past, and appreciating the present.

I began this book as a memoir, but as I was writing, it occurred to me that I may be able to serve as an example to others who surely have gone through similar situations but perhaps never realized their future self cannot be cast by others. They have that control firmly in their own hands. If they begin choosing wisely and acting with urgency, they, too, can achieve, and succeed, and chase their dreams of passion with passion.

To that end, I hope by sharing these stories of how I went from labor to leadership by shifting my belief system, my attitude, and my mindset that I can be an example! My hope is that others will start employing the discipline needed to make the changes permanent, and by trusting the systems and processes that I followed, which allowed me to grow as a person who understands that it is only by having the confidence to try new things and appreciate the *failures* as a sign that you are aiming high enough to make mistakes.

As the great Les Brown says, "The greater danger for most of us isn't that our aim is too high and miss it, but that it is too low and we reach it."

Part One: The Learning

Chapter 1: How Is Your Inlook?

I was brought into this world by two very young and damaged people. This led to the type of childhood with many mental and emotional lessons in store for me, just as you would expect from this type of upbringing in the 1970s.

What I didn't know at the time of my youth was there would one day be a moment so big that it would create a reckoning, a moment that would come from one single, drunken, slurred sentence, and would change me forever.

But before I forget, let me ask you this: do you exercise? When you work out, do you listen to music? Why do you listen to music? What kind of music do you listen to? Do you listen to Bob Marley and Jimmy Buffett? No, probably more like Rage Against the Machine or Slipknot! Why do you choose that kind of music? It's because you are adding external stimulus to get you in the right *mindset* for your workout, isn't it?

Should you need that stimulus, or should you be able to focus on your goal and be locked into the task? No one will deny the power of music and its short-term effect on your adrenaline levels and what it can help you do!

But what do you use to stimulate or motivate you to focus on your health, relationships, learning goals, and career?

Do you give up on things when you have a hard time understanding them or figuring them out, or when you get fatigued, or something better pops into your mind? Or do you get tunnel vision and refuse to put it down until you conquer it?

You see, for me, figuring out a brain teaser chain-link game my daughter gave me for Christmas isn't much different from figuring out the riddle that is the key to my battle with weight loss and anxiety eating or working on my reports until they are all completed, because doing so will ensure that every person working in my division is going to get paid for their efforts that week. This is even if it's during a hurricane, and I have to stay at it for 36 hours straight, because they deserve the pay, and I have to bill it. The difference between putting on loud, slamming music to get through your Zumba class and developing the action needed to succeed at whatever you want to achieve is drive and having the right mindset.

Your outlook and, more importantly, your inlook. Okay, I may have made that last word up, but it is this inlook that drives you. This is when you know what you want to achieve, and nothing can stop you until you complete that task, not even your own words yelling at you to stop. That is drive and mindset. Not seeing what others think they see in you but having your own inlook and buying in to what it can do.

Motivation is temporary, as David Goggins so eloquently states in his book *Can't Hurt Me*. David says that motivation will get you to strap on your running shoes, get your water bottles ready, and plan that two-mile run on your iPhone app. But what will you do when you open that door and it's raining, or snowing, or the weather isn't absolutely perfect? Ninety-nine percent of us would shut that door and be satisfied with the fact that you tried, and go back to sitting on the couch, knowing in your heart that there is always tomorrow. Because motivation only takes you so far.

To bust out another Ziglar-ism, "Motivation doesn't last. Well, neither does bathing. That's why we recommend it daily." Because it is an external additive. It's fake. But drive and inlook will make you continue out that doorway without even giving the elements a consideration. The goal is to run two miles. There are no obstacles that can stop you if you are driven.

Have you ever heard that it takes 21 days to create a new habit? Did you ever wonder where that saying came from?

It turns out that it was created by Dr. Maxwell Maltz, who is credited for starting the whole self-help book craze when he wrote *Psycho-Cybernetics* in 1960.

But before that, Dr. Maltz worked as a cosmetic surgeon in the 1950s, and he noticed a trend where his patients would report it took an average of 21 days to get used to their reflection in the mirror. Also, he worked with amputees, and he noticed they would have "phantom pain" for the same 21 days. This spread and perpetuated the myth that it takes 21 days to form a new habit.

However, getting used to seeing the results of a nose job or having a limb gone is quite different from changing a behavior. You have very little choice to go back into the old pattern with those examples.

Changing behaviors is a horse of a different color! We are here talking about changing deep-rooted, major, life-impacting issues like self-esteem, rage, and self-imagery. Heck, let's start off with something easier, like the behavior of coming home each night and eating half a bag of Cheese

Doodles while watching *Keeping Up With The Kardashians* and surfing your favorite social media app for three straight hours, looking for that instant hit of dopamine whenever anyone hits that "like" button on a post you made.

What if someone decided to change this routine? That would take real discipline! Changing the habit of craving instant gratification from the sugar of the Cheese Doodles, the likes and LOL's from the Facebook posts, the fast-forward button on your DVR to skip to the judges' scores on *Dancing with the Stars*...

Let us say that we change the Cheese Doodles to eating seven ounces of chicken and a fistful of broccoli instead?

How about exercising for 20 minutes straight every night instead of posting on Facebook?

And instead of watching the stars dance, we chase another star, your star, by reading every night or watching a YouTube video on a subject that may get you a promotion at work?

It wouldn't take much for someone starting to employ these new behaviors to slip right back into their old routine of junk food and TV, right?

This is why Dr. Maltz suggests that it actually takes 66 days on average to have the habit become automatic or routine.

After 66 days, you will not care about who or what Khloe and Kim are up to. You will be getting noticed at work by management because of your newfound knowledge of the real drivers that are creating your project's production, or because your writing skills have improved, or maybe your attitude will be evolving from why me? to can-do!

Success takes discipline! That's why TGIF is replaced with TGIS (The Grind Includes Saturday and Sunday) for those who know that discipline means making a full-time commitment.

So, how is your inlook? Are you focused on your mistakes, surroundings, family history, or past actions? Do you relive your failures over and over?

If so, stop, because this isn't inlook; this is living in the past. Inlook is seeing where you want to be, what you want to do, how you want to live and give, and from there, you figure out the why's. The how's and the when's will come from your why's, and you do not count the how much!

Chapter 2: Hard Knocks U

I do not sleep much. I call it insomnia, because it's faster and easier than explaining to everyone that I'm simply a bit crazy. I'm consumed with my passions, with my future, with my projects, and with my responsibilities. I am driven, and it's something I have in common with a hero of mine, a word I use sparingly.

Jocko Willink recently said this on the *Joe Rogan Experience* podcast:

People ask, "Why don't you sleep more?"

I answered, "Bro, I wish I could!"

I wish there wasn't a little thing in the back of my head going (whispering), "Hey, hey, you know you could be doing a lot more right now! What about this? What about that? What about the other thing?"

That's what's going on in my head.

There's not something in my head saying, "Gee, I haaave to get up."

No, there is a thing in there saying, "You better get up, you better get up. They are tracking you. They are watching you. You better get up. It's happening. There's a bad guy out there. He's training harder."

That's what's in my head.

Please, let the freaking powers of the world allow me to go into bed each night, and just pass out, and go, "I'm good. I'm satisfied with my life right now." I wish I could feel that for freaking eight hours a night.

It ain't there!

It ain't there!

It's like, "Oh, people talk about staying hungry. I'm freaking starving. I'm starving!"

Did I always have this inlook, this mindset, this drive, this constant need to improve? Absolutely not. It was quite the opposite. Back to that reckoning story...

I grew up dejected and rejected, with no self-esteem. I was jealous of those with low self-esteem. I was filled with rage. I fought probably 4-6 days a week from the time I was in 3rd grade until I was 17 years old. We lived in East Hollywood,

Florida, where I was born. I had parents who were alcoholics, drug users, and partiers. They were fun, I'll give them that, but there was no pride in my house, only humiliation the morning after, and getting up and out myself, and watching out for my sister and little brother because they needed me there. I considered myself a bully's bully. When I saw anyone picking on a weaker kid, I would step in and fight. I never allowed any of my friends to fight. I would elect myself to stand in for them during gang retaliations.

Luckily, even with all of the rage, I had a good heart. I even ended up becoming friends with a lot of the guys who are still alive from those days. I did have a few glimmering signs of hope in my head that there was something else or that this life could be better, but I had my sights set so low. This went on from as early as I can remember to well into my teens.

I did have happiness. I developed a great love of music. It stirred my soul. I was pretty good at drumming, and I was great at making my friends laugh. That was my talent. I hardly ever went to school. I had no interest in it at all. I was a terrible student. I felt like I had narcolepsy from sixth grade on. I would struggle to stay awake in class, often failing that fight and waking up to the bell in a puddle of drool. I didn't know it then, but I had dyslexia and ADHD. I couldn't sit still, and if I had to sit through a lesson I had no interest in learning, I would pass right out into a deep sleep. To this day, I can fall asleep anywhere but only for about 20 minutes!

I do not ever remember doing homework, never. I must have done just well enough on the tests I passed and went along from grade to grade. I only had to go to summer school once to get into high school. I know I averaged right around a 2.5 GPA, and that is only because the two subjects I loved took up half my day each year—Drumline/Band and ROTC.

I flourished in each of those classes, because for the most part I knew the instructor cared about my progress and my development. I communicated with the teachers, who seemed engaged, and I always felt like I wanted to live up to their expectations of me.

It may surprise you to learn that I never got to strut across the graduation stage to receive that holy grail, the high school diploma, a feat so high that in two generations, only my sister was able to achieve the exalted rank of high school graduate in the Torisk family. Part of the reason I didn't make it through the 11th grade was because I got suspended too many times for fighting and partly because I needed to get a job to support myself.

I left home at 17 to go be "on my own" because I figured it was better than being around the chaos and anger of my house. I say "on my own" because I still had a bed at my parents' apartment, and I stopped in to eat a lot. And to bathe, sometimes. But not long after I left my parents' place, they split up, and my family scattered away from South Florida. So, I was really on my own. I usually slept on the couch in the apartment of the girlfriend of my best friend Manny, but Manny and Vesta had a newborn baby, and that place ended up turning into another crazy-ass environment. Not that I didn't contribute to the fun. I was a nut. But it wasn't a long-term solution.

The only thing I missed from high school, besides playing the drums all afternoon with my friends in the marching band and playing grab-ass with the baton twirlers aka the Browardettes, was ROTC. Sergeant Major Ed Ruff was our ROTC teacher, and he was an *amazing man*. A man who led with passion and discipline. A man who had the confidence in his voice which could command attention from some very rowdy high schoolers. I loved the structure, and I wanted to have a place in the world that would give me that sense of security, and allow me to travel, and pay me for it! I decided to join the US Marine Corps. I was only 17, and that meant I was underage, but I heard about something called early enlistment.

I met Staff Sergeant Samuels at a recruitment center in Hollywood, Florida. He was a *mountain* of a man. He sat me down and asked me about my life. He drove me to my parents' house, where the paperwork was signed, and then we made the drive down to the testing center in Miami, where I took the ASVAB test. I wanted to be part of the Military Police. If I aced the test, this was my ticket out! So, I took the test and then immediately went through my first (and last) mass naked group physical. I will never forget that first, "turn your head and cough" moment. The kid next to me was being checked by another doctor. When he turned toward me with a look of utter humiliation, I couldn't help but laugh. After that, I went into the large "Red Room" and was sworn into service. I even received my dog tags that day! I remember I wouldn't take those off for anything!

Here is a photo of Manny Perez, me with my dog tags, and Benito Lazo circa 1988, complete with Little Manny's scribble on it for good measure.

Since I was only 17, I couldn't leave for boot camp for a year or so. I was supposed to do PT (military talk for Physical Training) with Staff Sergeant Samuels every weekend to get into boot camp shape, but on Saturday mornings I either had to work or I was passed out, because we were out at clubs until the sun came up. As a result, Sergeant Samuels was not aware that I had not gone back to school like I promised but instead had received my GED (general equivalency diploma). Passing that test was harder than if I had gone back to high school. I went to night school and had to study for the first time and pass a five-subject test. Drumline and ROTC were not on it anywhere! I did pass, though, on the first attempt!

Unfortunately, when I showed up to go to the infamous Parris Island, North Carolina for boot camp, I found out fast that a GED was not the same as a high school diploma in the eyes of the US government. So, the bus pulled off without me on it. And I have a hole in my heart until this very moment that I did not serve my government as a US Marine. It is a hole that will never be filled. It was my first real lesson that shortcuts never pay.

I was back at square one again, sleeping on Manny and Vesta's couch and working odd jobs like painting apartments for Manny's dad on weekends until Manny landed us a dream job! We started driving tow trucks for Cross Town Towing in Hallandale. Our buddy Richie Ferraro had the day job part of the deal. He did the 9-5 towing for gas stations and body shops, but Manny and I got to hang out at Hollywood Beach all day and all night seven days a week to tow cars to the impound yard when they didn't pay to park!

It was everything a rage-filled adolescent could ever ask for! Yes, I was *that* guy for about two years!

The best part about the job was that the impound yard was unmanned. This meant that when the owners would come up from a nice day or night out on the Hollywood Broadwalk (yes, it's called the Broadwalk in Hollywood) to find their car was no longer in its parking spot, they would eventually look around to see that they had to pay, and their car was towed. They would typically wait for us to come rolling back through the area, and when they spotted me, they would wave me down and ask if I had their car. When I told them yes and gave them the card with the address and a notice of the $110 fee to get their car out of beach jail, they would inevitably ask if I could give them a ride to the yard. I would always politely decline their request due to insurance regulations, and then I would wait for the next question which always came next, "Can you at least call me a cab?" My smirking reply was always the same, like I could hardly wait for the question to come out of their mouths: "Okay, you're a cab." Then I would speed off while rolling up my window!

Imagine their surprise when they pulled up to the yard in their cab, after hitting the ATM, of course, to see a locked gate and no booth. They would have to call the office, which would dispatch me to the yard to release their car. I would eventually show up with a car on the hook. This is where they usually mistook me for the complaint department! I really got great at fending off all types of name-calling and put-downs! Those people could be ruthless, but to me, they were paying me $45 to insult me! It was the most fun money I ever made! We could tow 20 cars a day from Friday to Sunday most weekends. For me, that was a lot of dough!

I really didn't have any professional aspirations of my own. I remember some people telling me throughout my teens that the way I talked with people was different, that I always saw sides to a problem that others didn't see at first, and that I should consider becoming a lawyer. Ha, ha, ha! That would be like telling me I should consider fighting Mike Tyson in Madison Square Garden, because I fought so much. It wasn't a thing! It was unimaginable. I knew where I was from and what I was made of. And worse, I had people who were supposed to love me tell me that I was nothing for most of my life. Every time I got into a fight, which was almost every day, I would hear, "That's just Jeremy."

Chapter 3: The Awakening

To this day, I have this vivid memory of a particular night when my sister and I were very young. At the time, I was about nine or ten years old, Paulette was probably ten or eleven years old, and our little brother Wesley would have been three years old or so. The three of us were lying on our little fold-up foam chair/bed about to go to sleep when Paulette looked at me and said out of nowhere, "Our dad isn't our dad." I couldn't grasp what she meant. I just laid there pondering what she could have been trying to say. "Our dad isn't our dad?" What could that mean? She went on to point out that she and I had blond hair like our mom, but our dad and Wes had dark hair, and all 5 of his sisters, his brother, and most of the 21 cousins on our dad's side of the family had dark hair. Our aunt Kathy and our cousins Sam and Travis, who were on Mom's side of the family, had blond hair like us. In addition, during Sunday dinners at our paternal grandmother's house, the whole family seemed to treat us differently. They didn't like us. But since my sister was deaf, I just figured that we all look at her differently. I learned how to communicate in a special way with Paulette, part American Sign Language and partly our own hand gestures. She read lips well. So, I told her she was being sensitive to them not talking with her as much. I blew it off, and we went to sleep. The truth of the matter is that because she was deaf, people had a tendency not to pay as much attention to what they said in her presence, and she picked up on a lot more than they probably realized at the time. We were street kids. And one thing that street kids do well is learn how to read a room. When you are raised around predators, you read body language exceptionally well.

Fast forward many years. I had just returned to Florida from attending my sister's wedding in Delaware. I was 20 years old, talking on the phone with my drunk grandmother. (Both of my grandmothers were perpetually drunk.) Grandma Brennan, my mother's mother, was telling me about how Joanne, my dad's new wife at the time, was at the rehearsal dinner with all the members from both sides of the family. My grandmother was outraged, because Joanne was openly complaining that it was crazy that she and my dad had to take time out of their lives to drive to a wedding four states away from their home in South Carolina, even though Paulette was not his daughter!

Boom! There it was. And there *I* was, instantly traveling through space and time. I was nine years old, lying in that cheap-ass foam bed in a small house in "Holly-hood" with my sister and brother, and she is saying *our dad is not our dad.*

In one moment, with one sentence, on that one phone call, it all made sense to me now.

All the dirty looks. All the snide remarks. All the belittling and feeling so different from the 21 cousins I had on my dad's side.

They were a Sicilian/Polish mixed bunch with dark hair and dark eyes, and dark and dank personalities. Never a positive word out of the whole clan. Not just to my sister and I, but as I recall, they all just reveled in the negative. I remember lots of laughter but always followed up by an insult, or a quip, or an eye-roll.

For years we had Sunday dinners, and I recall not really wanting to go. I just felt different there. Don't get me wrong. My cousins never did any of these things. Half of them were in the same boat, unbeknownst to any of us kids at the time. The difference was that my dad was the one raising my sister and I, and my mom put him through hell since they met in the fifth grade. She was (and continues to be) bat-shit crazy. I think that my dad's protective sisters all resented us for that. I am not angry with them now. I don't think they did it on purpose. They were just a loud group, unafraid to speak their minds, whether we were in the room or not. I felt stupid around them.

When my grandmother said those words to me over the phone that night about what Joanne revealed, I was living in my friend Brice's garage efficiency. I was standing in the doorway, and my girlfriend was facing me. She couldn't hear what was being said, but by the look on my face she assumed that maybe a fellow wedding goer had died on the way home or something equally tragic. I came to my senses and said, "I've got to go, Grandma."

I hung up the phone. I just remember standing, with that sentence repeating over and over in my head. The way my grandmother said it—so nonchalantly and with such contempt for Joanne for saying it. I was in shock. That memory is seared into my brain. After the shock wore off, I was trying to figure out what I was feeling. I finally realized that the two words which summed up what I was feeling were Yee Haw! You mean I have another person's DNA in my blood? I am *not* tethered to those people? I felt a huge sense of relief somehow. It was a true awakening! Now, I *love* my dad! But the family secret finally came to the light. Neither my sister nor I were his biological children. I told you, crazy life. And he *never, ever* mentioned it. And he *never, ever* showed that he even knew. *Ronald Anthony Torisk is our dad.* He always was and has continued to be our father in absolutely every sense of the word and every action he's ever displayed. He is one of a kind. But I felt like I had a whole new lease on life. I was not shackled to the names and low expectations that were always placed on me. I was not a Torisk. But what the hell does that mean? If I was not a Torisk, what was I?

I went on a mission to find my biological father. By that I mean I poked a lot of sleeping bears. I asked a lot of pointed and direct questions. I shook trees and upset a lot of apple carts. There was no internet in 1991, and there had been no communication between my mother and this man, who I later found out didn't live in Florida.

One day, I got a letter from my mom with a picture of her and a guy. They were both standing in a yard, beaming smiles in some '70s garb, with a house and some bushes right behind them, like they were getting ready to go to Easter Sunday services. On the back of the photo there was an imprint—July, 1970 (10 months before my birth).

In the letter, she rambled on about what went down on one of the many times she pulled a disappearing act while being with my dad, who she'd been with since middle school. Never mind that she did the same thing to him when she got pregnant with my sister who was born just 18 months prior (not fathered by the guy in the photo).

So, I called around the general area she claimed to have spent some time 21 years ago, and I searched high and low for some clarity. Somehow, I got the idea to call the schools in the town and ask if I could buy some yearbooks from 1965-1969. All I had was a partial name, a nickname that was shortened from the real name, like Dick is short for Richard. Well, I called the high school from the little town and, as luck would have it, I got the principal on the line. Luck was definitely on my side that day, as the principal had gone to school during those same years and knew a guy with that nickname! He even gave me the work number of the man in question. I stared at the number. And stared. And stared some more. The anticipation was overwhelming. This had been a long search that stirred up a lot of shit in my family. What was I going to say to this guy? Was I mad at him? Did he even really know? My mom wasn't exactly the best character witness. She had a lot of adventures in her life. And a lot of trauma. What was I about to put this man through? I dialed the number and held my breath as it rang.

When the secretary answered the phone, "Law Offices of Wei, Shcruuwem and Howe," I could have fainted!

He was a frickin' lawyer!

I was sooooo happpppyyyyy! I actually hung up the phone!

Not only was I cut free from the past, but I wasn't stupid!

I had *potential, lawyer potential!*

I never really "connected" with that man I will call Howe. I spoke with him exactly twice. I told him I was in my 20s and didn't need anything, but I wanted a friendship or, at a minimum, one lunch to see his face, his hairline, his smile, his mannerisms...if he was ever in Florida. Since his mother had retired and moved to southwestern Florida, he said he visited once a year or so and promised he would call on his next visit. That call never came. I was okay with that.

I needed the *mindset shift*. The *inlook had changed. I have lawyer DNA!* In one of my many attempts to look up Howe online to see what he looked like; I came across his obituary. Thank you, Howe, for my lawyer DNA!

Chapter 4: The Growing

I awoke the next morning with an unfamiliar bounce in my step. I had always enjoyed working, as it was the only surefire way to elicit a compliment such as, "Wow, looks good, Jeremy," or "What a hard worker you are, Jeremy!" or my favorite from my Aunt Pat White, "Good job, Charlie Brown." I always loved hearing people say nice things about my efforts, but on this day, I had an inner peace about my place. I didn't look for the compliment after the job. I noticed that when anyone asked me, "How is it going?" or "How are you?" I would snap back a grin and say, "Great!" I have continued that throughout my life. No matter the mood, no matter the situation, whenever anyone asks me how my day is going, I instantly smile and say, "Great! How is your day?" My mindset had been altered.

When I lived from my memory, I focused on the past, on the names people called me, on the labels they assigned to me. They wanted me to fail, and I bought in for years. I used to tell myself how shitty I was, how dumb I was, how ugly I was. But because of that fateful phone call when I learned that my DNA wasn't connected to that prison sentence, that I could have control, I lived from my imagination. I freed myself from those beliefs, and I shifted my focus to the future. I didn't realize it at the time, but it was "textbook" Stephen Covey!

Stephen Covey says, "What lies behind us is nothing compared to what lies *within* us and ahead of us." That is part of Rule # 2, Begin with the End in Mind, in *The 7 Habits of Highly Effective People*. In that book Stephen writes, "You need to listen, reflect and remember and then imagine, refocus, redefine and reorganize. Then write your problems in the sand, because they are temporary." Stephen advises us to ask, "What are our unique gifts? Do we listen to those who see the potential in us? Do we study the lives of people who inspire us?"

I didn't know any of the answers that night. I just knew that what I had been through to that point did me a service, because when I looked to see where my friends were in that stage of our lives, we pretty much were at the same place— just out of school and starting to think about what we were becoming. However, now I felt like I could step into the starting blocks with everyone else, only I was the one with the advantage.

The way I saw it, they were complacent, because that day was just like any other in their lives. But I truly felt energized by the potential for which I never gave myself credit.

I realized that I was not the only one who saw that potential in me. My small group of friends had always tried to tell me, but I didn't believe them. My girlfriend's family also saw something in me, and it was right about that time I got the offer that would kick off my 30-year career.

They say that life is about the journey, not the destination. It is on the journey that these amazing moments occur which cause our perspective to shift just enough to cause the path to change course by only a degree or two, but over time, that small shift can lead to a totally different destination than you were heading toward or you thought you deserved.

What have been some defining moments from your life that you can use to change your mindset? Ones that can open your mind to accepting that you are at the wheel, that you are writing the script, and that script can have as many acts as it takes for you to succeed and improve your life?

Chapter 5: Hustle While You Wait

My very first promotion came because of that need for constant movement and proactive mindset. It wasn't purposeful; it was natural. I felt emboldened. It was like my rage was channeled into productive action.

At that time, I was working in a combustion engine repair shop grinding welds for just over minimum wage, around $4.25 per hour. I used to bring home about $160.00 per week, with some overtime and after paying Uncle Sam.

I actually liked it a lot. The boss and his wife were very nice to me, and I loved my coworkers. But unless I wanted to become a welder, it was a dead-end job. The idea of becoming a welder seemed like a great trade, but it also seemed to be a very meticulous and repeatable routine. There was no way I could have handled a monotonous job. At the time, I still had ADHD, a diagnosis that would not occur until I was 40 years old. So, no, I never considered welding combustion chambers as an option.

In 1991, my girlfriend's mom and her boyfriend instantly saw the shift in me, however. Sandy and Shannon ran a small subcontracting company for a man named Charlie Yecker.

The customer was a regional cable company in Pompano Beach, Florida.

Shannon offered me a job making double what I was making at the combustion shop in Hollywood, to which I immediately responded, "Yes. *Hell, yes!*" I didn't even ask what I'd be doing. I just knew it would double my income. On top of that, they allowed me to move into the house and pay half the rent I was paying for the efficiency in Hollywood. This allowed me to buy an old beater Honda to get to work on my own! They literally and figuratively put me on the road to success!

Little did I know that my job would be digging pits on either side of a driveway so that the "missile crew" could place a conduit under the driveway, and the cable installer could replace the bad cable feeding a house with the service issue. It was *hot, hard work*. Even though Florida has all that green grass, where I worked coral rock lay just 3 inches under all that lush topsoil, and the directive was to place the new cable 18 inches underground.

I rarely complained; I worked!

When it rained, I worked.

When it was the weekend, I worked.

I just worked.

And when the holidays came, I worked.

I had no family to visit and no kids to raise.

I kept my head down, and I worked!

Eventually I was pulled off "pit duty," and I graduated to installer. The cable company used us subcontractors, because the in-house guys complained about the hot attic work and digging in the cable to the houses.

There was a catch, though. I needed a truck. As luck would have it, I happened to be talking to my Aunt Carol, and I mentioned that I was looking for a truck. She said, "Well, you know your cousin Paul is looking for a car to trade his old truck for!" I couldn't believe it. He actually wanted my car! I traded my cousin Paul the Honda Accord for his Nissan pickup truck. Of course, I still feel badly, because a week later the serpentine belt went out on the Honda, but that Nissan purred like a kitten for years.

Even though I had been digging pits for a year and now I was actually working with the cable, I still had my rookie

31

stripes on. Digging pits does not afford you any rank among the senior guys. So, I was at the bottom of the dog pile.

Each morning all of the installers and laborers would show up in the warehouse parking lot early. Although the bay doors would be open, the bosses wouldn't come out with our assignments until after their morning brief. So, we all just milled around, waiting for our routes.

I could not stand listening to the same talk every day about who drank more beer the night before or who sucked at their jobs more. To get away from those fuckers, I used to sweep. I'd grab a broom every morning and sweep the warehouse floor. I did this to escape the chest-thumping, but I didn't realize I was being noticed. I did it every day, and nobody asked me to do it. I just did it for me. I couldn't stand the negative talk every morning from the senior dogs.

About two months went by when an MDU (multiple dwelling units, such as apartments, condominiums, and townhouses) route became available. These typically went to senior installers, because it didn't involve attic work or subfloor crawling, and you were usually done by 2 PM, still earning about the same money. All the MDU installers would get together with the MDU construction crews, who also tended to wrap up just after lunch, to head to a lake near the shop in Pompano Beach and go jet skiing every afternoon. The construction guys were another group of chest-thumpers, but at least they had fun together.

On this day, Shannon called me into his office and offered me the MDU route. Since there were other senior guys there, I was surprised, but not as surprised as Shannon when I asked if I could keep my SFU (single family units) route and add this new MDU route to it! He asked why I would do that. I said, "Well, I see the guys on the MDU crew. They usually get done early and go jet skiing every afternoon, but I need to grind, and if I can work a little harder, I am sure I can run both routes." Shannon shook his head and said, "Fat chance" but agreed to let me try.

The first two weeks were a dumpster-fire. Everything went wrong. I was out until 9:30 PM each night, and the complaints for missing appointment windows were stacking up. But then something just clicked. I was prioritizing calls, calling ahead to make sure that the tasks on the work order were what the customer really needed so I could route myself more efficiently. I excelled at those routes for almost a year, and every morning, while waiting for my routes in the parking lot, I swept.

After a while, I asked to be switched to the MDU construction division if the opportunity ever presented itself. I wanted a change and to learn more about building the plant instead of just hooking the customers up to it.

Eventually, one opened, but I was passed over. This happened again. I was passed over a few more times when I finally asked why I wasn't being considered for the MDU construction crews. Shannon said that he couldn't afford to lose my production on the installation side. I had actually worked too hard and pigeonholed myself!

The way I saw it, I had a choice. I could start sucking at my job, or I could quit and go look for work doing something else. I chose the second option. I was totally honest about it. I asked Shannon for a day off so I could go get my CDL (commercial driver license). My dad had always driven a truck, and it seemed to be a lot easier than crawling around attics in South Florida during the summer…or any time, for that matter. I was given the day off, and I got my CDL. I actually had to drive an 18-wheeler for the test. All of a sudden, I wished I was in an attic! At least I wouldn't kill anyone with this freakin' tank! It was stressful! But after I worked another week, I asked for another day off to go apply for truck driving positions around the city. As luck would have it, I got a call that night and was informed that a position had just opened on the MDU construction crew. Guess who they offered it to? That's right, *me*!

My proactiveness got me that promotion. I used open, direct, and respectful communication, and it was done with transparency. It paid off. And every day that I worked on that MDU construction crew, I swept.

After about eight months, without requesting it, I was promoted to MDU Construction Supervisor. That meant I needed to get into the office early to prep the work for the different teams, but I was still a Construction Tech, too. The job came with a small raise, but when I got my first check, it also had a $500 bonus! When I called the office to find out what the bonus was for, they said, "Charlie said it was his way of thanking you for sweeping the floors for all that time."

I never knew he even noticed, and when I saw Charlie to thank him, he told me that all of my promotions, from the first one to the most recent one, was due to my willingness to pick up the broom and sweep, no matter what my job title was over the years, without anybody having to ask me. I hadn't realized I was given that MDU route opportunity because I swept the floors each morning without looking for anything in return. This opened that first door and got the owner's attention. And when he heard that I was looking for a job elsewhere instead of being put on the MDU construction crew, he almost fired Shannon for passing me up all of those times! That will learn ya!

It is precisely that proactive mindset that makes you act. Asking questions and doing jobs without being told. Doing things for yourself. That really sets you apart from 90% of your so-called competition. At the end of the day, the competition takes place in your head!

I always say that I wasn't the smartest guy on the team, or the most technical guy, and *definitely* not the most liked guy, but *no one* was going to outwork me. And that is from having a proactive mindset.

Chapter 6: The Corporate Ascent Begins

Eventually I worked my way up to a splicing position, which meant I was splicing main-line coaxial cable directly with the cable company technicians and supervisors on a huge upgrade which was projected to last for one year. They immediately took a liking to my work and my can-do attitude. They saw that I didn't complain about anything; I just did the work. A man named Wayne Ingram ran the upgrade team, and a supertech named Keith Holland told him about me. Wayne asked me to lunch to see if I wanted to join the company.

I was flabbergasted but conflicted! I felt such loyalty to Shannon and Charlie, but I had since married Laurel, and she was pregnant with our first son, Trace. Shannon and Charlie both knew I was better off working in-house for the cable company with the mega health benefits, longevity potential, and unlimited room to grow. They asked me if I wanted to be "a big fish in a little pond or a little fish in a big pond." I said I knew I wouldn't stay little for long in that big pond, and they agreed. That was a very hard decision, and I thank Atlantic Cable and Company for everything you did for me!

On July 21, 1997 I joined MediaOne (formerly Continental Cable, formerly American Cable, formerly…) as a high-level splicing technician. The department was a specialty unit, where I was able to make a name for myself. But that name was not one I wanted! My contractor work habits and natural drive did not align with my lifelong clock puncher coworkers. I did roughly three times the production of most of them and found out really quickly that you cannot talk to the in-house guys the same way you can to a subcontractor! Oh, the skin was thin, my friends! I had to adjust my mean-mug (which is called "resting bitch face" these days) and throttle back on my expectation that everyone was just as enthusiastic about doing all that could be done in a day. I realized that most of these guys had no real incentive to do the maximum amount of work possible. Their check would be the same amount no matter what they put out in effort each week. Although my efforts were for my own satisfaction, being a contractor all those years and making more money each week as my performance would allow made me forget what it was like to punch a clock. I finally figured out how to get along with these guys. They were true professionals. I came in with my contractor mentality—

moving 100 mph. When I learned how to temper my excitement, we all settled into an elite group.

After about a year as a splicer, an opening came up for a supervisory position. The upgrade had spread to Hialeah, a town in northwest Miami, and a supervisor was needed to run the splicing team. I saw this as an opportunity both to grow in responsibility and to stretch this project out another year. I applied and nailed it! I was promoted to Upgrade Supervisor and placed in another position of dealing with guys who had worked in that system for over a decade. Again, I was the outsider who needed to manage a crew of men, and I had never been taught how to command respect. So, again, I fought the system and lost until I got some advice from an old-timer permit coordinator who said, "You can catch more flies with honey than with vinegar." I was very apprehensive, but I tried it, and it seemed to work. I didn't give into every demand, but I started letting go of the reigns slightly. I gave some authority to the guys to set their own targets and allowed them to switch to a 10-hour workday, cutting out a day if they hit their targets. It worked, and I got my first taste of success. The Hialeah group regularly beat the pants off my old Pompano Beach group. And once again, without trying to, I was noticed.

Within about a year, I was called into a director's office and met by a few new faces. We had merged with yet another company and were then called AT&T Broadband. I was told that our two regions, Pompano Beach and Hialeah, were merging with another cable company, formerly called TCI, and their Broward, Miami-Dade, and Florida Keys regions were all going to make one gigantic region called South Florida. AT&T Broadband had constructed a building in Miramar, Florida, which resembled a Supermax prison, to run a massive $80 million upgrade that was slated to last four years. And I was named Upgrade Manager for Miami-Dade County and the Florida Keys! I was probably one of the youngest managers in the company at the time, responsible for watching over a $40 million construction upgrade, with 24 employees and 40 contractors under my charge.

Was I ready for any of that? *Hell, no. I was not.* But I was getting my *reckoning*! Not with negativity or anger, but with *love, love* for myself! I would show all of those in my past that I was not how they saw me; I was an achiever!

I made plenty of mistakes, pissed off a lot of people, and I probably could have done a million things better, but with each failure, I smiled! I like failure. That isn't to say I *want*

40

failure or I don't regret failure. I do. But I *never let it get me down* because of what I have overcome to be here, and I have still further to go.

And then, seemingly as soon as it all happened, it changed again. The AT&T Broadband experiment I was really getting deep into had just been bought by Comcast! At the time it was the largest acquisition by what was then a very small cable company. This move catapulted Comcast from basement dwellers in the telecommunications world to one of the top three with a stroke of a pen and a shitload of money—ironically enough, money obtained from AT&T for *not* bidding on the MediaOne and TCI companies against AT&T! AT&T actually paid Comcast to stay away from the bidding table. Comcast wisely invested the payment, waited, and then bought AT&T Broadband with basically their own money after just two years!

At the time, I reported to my first real mentor, Nestor Martin. Nestor was my first real father figure, also. It was a source of pride to succeed in order to make someone else successful! I wanted to do the best I could so Nestor would get the praise of running this behemoth of a company! Nestor shared personal stories of his experiences when he recognized my struggles. It was a very good tactic, as I would always want to try harder not to repeat the mistakes which had caught Nestor's eye.

When Comcast came to town, they brought in a new Regional Vice President named Filimon Lopez. This guy was a charismatic leader who believed in documented training programs, because he had come from developing the training curriculum for the Comcast corporate office in Philadelphia.

It was *mandatory* for all managers and above to go to Philly for a week to partake in a learning annex called "Leading the Broadband Way." This is where I had my first exposure to real corporate style leadership training, and I fell in love with it! I made fast friends with the local training department in south Florida and frequently volunteered to speak with new hires about my department and our role. I also helped every chance I could to formalize some training with the technical team.

Filimon is directly responsible for opening my eyes to the love of learning and the power of the motivational mindset. He would gather the south Florida Managers routinely for offsite group meetings. He had great music pumping over the speakers and gave amazing speeches. He brought in professional athletes and coaches like Dan Marino, Alonzo Mourning, and Coach Pat Riley to speak with us! He scheduled mass cooking lesson competitions and yacht outings, where we would have dance-offs! Filimon was the guy who took everyone from TCI Broward, TCI Dade, TCI Monroe, American Cable, Continental Cable, and Media One and made us all Comcasters! A family with one goal— the customer experience and growing our brand. He created an environment that allowed true interdepartmental bonds with managers that I am proud to say I still have to this day.

Because of Filimon, I started reading motivational books. I had never even read one book in high school, but before I knew it, I was reading one book per month! One of the early books I read was written by Stephen Covey, and it really hit home for me. It talked a lot about a proactive mind. That is what switched on for me that night all of those years ago. When I found out about my lawyer DNA, I became proactive instead of reactive, which I had been my whole life!

They say the proactive mindset involves "being aware of what you want out of life and the kinds of behaviors that are important to get there." It promotes the ability to recognize things you can control and ignore the things you can't control.

One way to know when you have chosen to act with the proactive mindset and shifted into having a naturally proactive mentality is when you notice your actions are much like those of a shark. It's all about continuous movement and eliminating the very thought of needing to be told to do something before doing it. It is precisely this mindset that was responsible for my success over the years.

Let's see where you are with your mindset.

Do you have a job or a trade?

If you don't know, you need to examine what you are doing with your time. Figure out what you want out of life and, as Tony Robbins says, *"make your move!"*

Here are some things you can start doing to get your proactive on!

1. Learn about your profession on your own after-hours, often called continuous education.

2. You can get up early to plan your day and organize your thoughts.

3. You can exercise regularly, just 20 minutes, and you don't need weights or a gym!

4. You can count your blessings. Make gratitude lists.

5. You can read daily. It doesn't matter what you read as long as it's not social media, but books are best.

6. You can be proactive in your communication about your career path with your bosses by asking *them* what you can do to improve your chances for promotion.

Here are some knee-jerk responses you should listen for to get clues about your present state of mind:

Current language	Replace with
That's just the way I am	I can choose a different approach
There's nothing I can do	Let's look at our alternatives
He makes me so mad	I control my own feelings
I can't	I choose
I must	I get to
If only	I will

None of these things can be done for the sole purpose of getting you to the next level or for the attention. Your motivation has to be organic and sincere. It must be done only because you prefer moving over sitting and putting yourself out there. You will risk stumbling and perhaps failing, but you'll never learn anything from sitting.

I hope this message will inspire you to acknowledge your past and admit your shortcomings but also to imagine your future and redefine your legacy. And when you dream, dream big. But get up and *chase them*!

I am going to end this chapter with a quote from Henry Ford. "Whether you think you can, or you think you can't, you're right."

Chapter 7: J Ain't Right

When I was in my mid-20s, I took up martial arts (American Kenpo), and with every kick to the stomach and punch to the face, I would smile. They started calling me "J ain't right," because I would just smile when the pain crossed my body, and I didn't even know I was smiling. But I was thinking, "I'm still standing, and you, with your black belt and years of training, couldn't get me down." Well, I got knocked down a lot, but I would always get back up smiling, and they would yell, "J ain't right!" By then, that was my mindset. I. AM. DRIVEN.

I did not know I was capable of any of these things before that call from my grandmother, though. Up to that point in life I was in a dark cocoon. I had no vision of gaining respect from others or thinking I was capable of anything more than maybe driving a truck. Outwardly, though, my rage took care of the facade. I was always looking for a reason to fight. I had a knack for finding bullies and making eye contact. That is usually all it took to push a bully into showing his true colors. They'd buck-up or mouth-off, and I would clock them! I had zero tolerance for that whole chest-to-chest talkin' shit phase that kids used to do back in the day. When someone called me out, I would come out swinging. It was for this reason people thought I had tons of confidence. This was actually shame in disguise.

You see, when you have low self-esteem, you actually protect it. You do not take chances for people to say, "I told you so." So, you become reactive by nature.

But when you do not look to others for your happiness or approval, failing takes on a whole new shine! When you learn that failure is progress, and people point to those failures as reasons to stop, this is a sign that those people need to be out of your life! Now I said, "How big can I fail?" I failed so often that eventually I was even failing upwards!

Meaning that later in life, when I would experience my *biggest, ugliest failures*, when I would land *flat on my back*, I was still higher than where I was with my old mindset. Because this is America, buddy! You don't get just one bite of the apple. It's all you can eat! As Les Brown said, "If you are looking up from your back, you can get back up!"

"J ain't right" is how I can push through each *no* without showing any signs of stopping. It is how I can be resilient, because I know my failures are leading to better situations.

And it is how I was able to meet the woman I am married to today in one of the darkest periods of my professional and personal adult life without presenting that defeatist, woe-is-me attitude that would have *repelled* a woman like Christy in one second flat! When life served one of the biggest gut kicks I had ever received, I was smiling through it.

I had survived poverty, a variety of abuse, and the tragic suicides of my brother Wesley and later, my brother-in-law Rick as well as the untimely death of by beautiful beloved cousin Sam (Deet-Deet). Since I was the patriarch of my family, I had a huge role in rallying the troops, scheduling funerals, and gathering family who had scattered across the eastern United States, to reconnect and turn these tragedies into celebrations and epic reunions that still are cherished to this day, by me at least.

So, when the biggest defeating and defining period of my professional and personal adult life occurred, I had to rely on every win I had ever experienced to give me the strength to come through it.

When the rebuild came to an end, almost six years after my one-year plan had started back in 1999, I was looking at two options. One was a lead technical training position with

Comcast. It was considered a lateral move that I would have been great at. But I knew myself too well and felt like I would lose myself in solely training others the ABC's of CATV.

I opted for door number two. A generous offer from a long-time subcontractor called CCU in Miami. For 25 years they had a stranglehold on the Dade County CATV construction scene, and rightly so. They worked hard for it. But at that time, there was an opportunity in the West Palm Beach market. It seems an old, familiar name who had left Comcast some time ago was running an upgrade. His name was Nestor Martin. That's right. My mentor.

CCU appointed me with my first directorship and allowed me to venture into the West Palm Beach market with the CCU brand and use my relationship to build a business. Do you know what they say about timing? It is everything!

The year was 2005, and from July 9th to October 24th, south Florida was under threat of or slammed with four hurricanes. Hurricanes Dennis, Katrina, Rita, and Wilma all impacted us from Key West to Martin County. For us, Hurricane Wilma caused the most damage, since the CATV systems were already bandaged and barely standing from the previous storms. But for a newly formed unit in a market that we had never served, this time allowed us to grow as a company exponentially. The windfall allowed me to have real money for the first time in my life.

As life often goes, you rarely get to have your cake and eat it, too. So, as my business life was successful, my marriage of 10 years was coming to a conclusion. My wife and I were going through a mutual and friendly divorce. The money I was earning allowed us to pay off our debt including our children's college funds. I eventually got into a nice home and maintained a true friendship with Laurel, because throughout the entire process, the kids came first.

Following the storms, I settled into my new single daddy business running routine. I created a great niche in the market working on "new build" properties assigned to CCU from the cable company. This meant that we had crews placing fiber and cable systems in brand-new developments all over the West Palm Beach market. I was doubling the business every few months; so, every week I was buying machinery, trucks, and tools, as well as hiring people. Of course, this was almost all on credit.

But in December 2009, the housing market bubble finally burst. I had six projects all shut down just weeks before

Christmas. I kept hoping that the projects would come back before long, so I used up all of my savings to keep from losing my employees and ruining my credit. By March of 2010, I had lost a business which had 19 employees, and it eventually drove me to into bankruptcy.

At 40 years old, I was literally alone and broke. But for the lengthy foreclosure process at the time, I was staring at not knowing where I would live. Just 18 months prior I was on top of the world! But when I stood back and examined the previous five years, I had actually failed at the marriage to my sons' mother, and committed countless self-inflicted ignoramus decisions, and made many inappropriate or mistimed comments. I had many alcohol-fueled binges and bar fights as a grown man, and trashed meaningful relationships with kind people who genuinely loved me.

I can honestly say that there are more than a few major regrets. But… "J ain't right."

These mistakes would not prevent me from moving onward and upward, and I can look *everyone* I have ever known or crossed paths with square in the eyes with open arms and love, because I am better for those experiences. I am driven. I am smiling. And I will succeed.

Chapter 8: B-Positive and To-Risk

It was my 40th birthday. I was sitting in a house that I wasn't able to pay for any longer. I was on my couch, because I couldn't climb the staircase to the bedroom due to recent surgery to repair a massive knee injury as a result of engaging in something I had no business being a part of. Due to a calendar mix-up, my kids' flag football team showed up to a game that had no opponent. So, some of the fathers decided to play against our football team of 12-year-olds. On the first play of the game, I collided with an 85-pound kid. Rather than careening over him with my 275 pounds, I made a very awkward move to try to soften some of the blow to the kid. *Snap!* I tore my right knee to pieces. You name it, and I tore it.

I had *no* job, *no* money, *no* prospects. My fiancée of four years had recently moved out. I had dwindled my $60,000 safety net to *zero,* and I was more than $20,000 behind in my child support. Oh yeah, I only had a 10th grade education and a GED.

One day, I received an email claiming that I could earn money selling health and life insurance and annuities if I just had a 415 state license. I drove all the way to Orlando to an "interview," and they helped me apply for a two-week class near my home to qualify me to take the state exam. After the class concluded, I tried signing up to take the state exam only to learn that due to a little thing like being tased by the police and arrested just a year earlier for fighting five Florida Gator college students in a Gainesville bar before a Miami Hurricane game disqualified me from being permitted to hold such a license. Luckily, since it was my first legal experience since I was 19, the charges were eventually dropped, and all I had to do was provide the documentation.

As soon as I received my license I began "dialing for dollars" selling life and health insurance! I actually made sales, too! I felt that I truly was helping people find the best policies to fit their family's needs and budgets. I found that I had a knack for getting strangers to trust my advice and direction. I never sold a policy based on commission, even as broke as I honestly was. I put the client's needs first, but I also learned how to not count their money. Meaning that even if I thought the premium was "high," if that served them best, I would simply state the facts and allow them to decide if it fit within their budget. This little tactic holds so many salespeople back from true success.

Even though I was selling a decent amount of health insurance plans, Obamacare was staring me right in the face, and I read the message loud and clear. The health insurance game was changing very soon, and the game was almost over. Eventually, I ended up with a group of really high energy folks who were selling life insurance with Primerica when they were still a private corporation. I really took to the owners of this group, a husband and wife team named Brett and Andrea Burks, who were extremely inspiring and motivating. I really did give it my all for almost a year. But the Primerica business plan is built on one thing, and that is having a team under you. So, I started to build a team. But in the meantime, I still had child support stacking up month after month. Ironically enough, I was responsible for providing the health insurance for my boys. I needed an income while I built this team.

The business was located in a complex that was anchored by a huge call center. We had a lot of those call center people showing up after their shifts who wanted to break into the industry as a team member of other people's teams. I was one of the oldest new guys with the Primerica gang and had a lot of life experience. So, I would often be asked to get up and speak to the group. I love speaking; so it was always a

56

thrill to tell the gang about a recent situation that I had to overcome to close a sale or to just inspire someone to keep trying for that first sale. That is where I came up with, "I do not have give up in my DNA; I welcome *no's* and the word *next*. My blood type is B(Positive), and my last name is To-Risk!"

One of those team members told me that the call center was in a hiring frenzy, they were growing fast, and offered great benefits. That's all I needed to hear. I was feeling like a deadbeat dad, and I needed to turn my income situation around.

I walked in and asked for an application. I sat in the lobby with the dozen or so others and completed the paperwork there and then. When I turned it in, I mentioned that I was referred by an agent. The receptionist scrawled the agent's name across the top and promised I would hear from someone soon.

I actually did hear from someone within a day or so, and I made my appointment for an interview, one of seven rounds of interviews! I guess I threw them off kilter when I asked if I could earn $120,000 per year with this company. During the first of the real interviews, I met Vince Salerno. Vince was in charge of the entire call center agent floor. All of the departments rolled up under Vince. I learned that the company sold home services over the phone with both incoming and outgoing calls. I asked what home services they offered, and he told me they represented companies such as Comcast, Verizon, Dish Network, and ADT home security, just to name a few.

I had never sold anything before, except my abilities to outperform what people's expectations of me were. Even when I was helping people find health insurance, I never thought of myself as a salesperson. I was simply helping people cover their family's future and protecting their savings.

I told Vince that I had many different attributes that would make me a great salesperson, though. I had worked for the cable company for most of my adult life, and I would be able to really connect with the product. Selling health and life insurance during the past year gave me a feel for when to go for the close. I had been developing a team to work for me; so, I knew I could work well with others. Also, I told him how I was a fighter and didn't mind working crazy long hours. That is when I "pulled a Jeremy." Vince was a very large man at the time and very pale, too. I said I knew they put in the hours here, because living in south Florida, you should have more color, even if was just from walking to and from the car to the office during daylight hours. He was speechless and just shook his head. Years later Vince told me that no one had ever insulted him so boldly during an interview, but it was just so funny and true.

With all my combined skills and experience, he suggested that I may be interested working in a new division the company had created. It wasn't selling product; it was selling a platform to sell the products from home. They called it "Business in a Box," and it was essentially a glorified referral program that actually paid great commissions.

I loved the idea, and after four more interviews, I was offered a supervisory position. However, I couldn't tell anyone until I learned about the product and how to sell it over the phone. I asked for $70,000 and settled for $45,000. Talk about a difficult decision. I needed the insurance, and I knew I could grow with the opportunity.

On my first day I was supposed to shadow a phone agent and take in the flow and process. After about 20 minutes on the floor, I was listening to an agent presenting the opportunity to a prospect. They were following the script and hitting the marks but not getting a credit card number. We happened to sit right in front of Vince's office, and he could hear everything this team was doing. Vince walked up and said, "Pass the call to Jeremy." I was dumbfounded, but what could I say? The agent passed her headset to me and clicked the reconnect button. I was numb. I said, "Hello there, Mr. Smith. I am Jeremy Torisk, and I hear that you have some questions about the program. I can answer them for you. May I ask if you are more concerned about how many sales you are allowed to make every week, or is it about how much support you will be given to grow your business?" We spoke for about eight more minutes before I finally ended the call without the credit card number.

Vince gathered the team and introduced me as the divisional supervisor. This took me by surprise, because this was supposed to be kept quiet as I gained some experience, and I didn't make the sale! When I asked Vince why he revealed the plan so quickly, he told me the action I took and the questions I asked told him all he needed to know. Sales is not something you can get good at by reading scripts. It is about making connections and turning prospects into relationships.

Per my usual MO, I put in the long hours. I worked open to close six days a week. I learned everything I could about the product, how phone CRMs work, how to interview and hire real go-getters instead of salespeople. I created new KPIs (key performance indicators) with my Excel skills and learned how to run reports that actually showed where we needed to improve. I gave constant feedback to the agents that let them know where they excelled and what needed to be worked on. I eventually was promoted a number of times and reached the title of Director. This was a very pivotal occurrence in my life, because after reaching this level, I was moved from the call center floor into the executive suite. I had an office, and I was in all of the important meetings, which helped me connect with all of the company decision-makers.

There was a great perk in the executive suite, too. Once a week they brought in a really hot barber to cut the executives' hair. I reported to James Flynn at the time, and, as usual, I had my face firmly glued to my laptop screen when James popped into the office and said, "The haircut lady is here," then flashed his big Texas grin. I had heard of the hot barber lady. So, I looked in my pockets and came up with a $20 bill for the customary tip. It was my last $20 for the week, and it was Tuesday. I decided that I needed to fast anyway and headed into the executive bathroom to meet Christy.

As she cut my hair, I couldn't help flirting with her, and eventually we discovered we lived just five minutes from each other! I asked if she would want to grab a drink sometime, and she said yes! That friendship eventually grew into a courtship and, lucky for me, a beautiful marriage. Yes, the Queen of South Florida Real Estate was a barber! And a damn fine one, too!

But alas, nothing lasts forever. After a few years learning about marketing and lead generation, and serving some amazing people at that company, two of whom I consider mentors to this day, change was afoot.

I was still not making the money I needed; so, I decided I wanted to get back into the telco-construction game again. After all, the economy was picking back up, and this was the field in which I had intimate knowledge.

I had a contact at SBA Towers, who told me they were hiring a project manager for their cell tower builds. I reached out to the company I worked for after I left Comcast to ask for a reference and, coincidentally, they had started a sister company which worked on cell towers at a national level and needed a project manager. They asked if I would consider the opportunity, which included extensive traveling. After discussing it with my ex-wife and kids, who were about 10 and 13 at the time, I decided to accept.

That move was very significant, as it led to me walking into a mess. The company had over $300,000 in open invoices due to poor tracking and documentation. I had to learn to run multiple crews across multiple states and about the unbelievably complicated cell tower industry closing package process. It took about six months, but I closed out all of the open jobs. Eventually, I started billing $200,000 a month in new work, which was paid in a timely manner as well as being profitable. Later, I was asked to head to Texas to save the fledgling AT&T account. Again, they were behind on getting paid and growing a reputation for being late with their aerial project deliverables.

When I came to town, I saw the local guys were doing a great job, but they had no consistency when it came to the crews turning in and documenting their work. I put in place a lot of the processes I had learned in the cell tower industry and ended up turning that around in about two months. We went from billing $20,000 per month to $500,000 per month.

That is when I was reunited with an old comrade named Wes Parsons. I had known Wes since our children were in preschool together, almost 20 years prior. Wes was my travel/battle buddy! Wes and I put some major miles in the air over a three-year period! He and I made an unbeatable team.

When the underground work began in the Dallas area, Wes' connections and relationship skills, combined with my hard-driving and consistent process, were pivotal in getting us to grow the revenue to over $4,000,000 per month. That's right. Consistent revenue of *one million dollars per week*.

I stayed with the company until the fall of 2019, when I was a victim of a political power move. Wes Parsons left the company and began a consulting firm amidst some disagreements with the ownership.

The company was transitioning when a hurricane struck the Florida Keys. They put me in charge of the on-the-ground efforts in Key West. I made a few calls and had over 100 contractors under my charge within two weeks. Rebuilding after hurricanes is my specialty. I thrive in chaos!

During the restoration process, there was an allegation made that I may have been helping Wes with his business. After six years and countless efforts to save the company, I was fired one week before Thanksgiving. No severance package, no bonus, which was arguably in the low six figures.

Was I worried? No. Not for one minute. I took a week and spent it with my family. I decided to follow Wes' lead and consult. I connected with an old friend named Les Smith. He was working for Wes Parsons in the islands. Les invited me to help them following the two category 5 hurricanes which ravaged Puerto Rico and the Virgin Islands.

I ended up working in the islands for over a year, and it was truly *the most rewarding* year of my life. Restoring the telephone and cable systems on those islands and living among everyone else without power, or air conditioning, or traffic controls, or street signs, or coffee, and leading my crews amidst these surreal surroundings was an experience and a source of pride that no one can ever take from me.

After a year in the Caribbean, we came back to the mainland and started reconnecting with our clients. We took the lessons learned from all of our collective pasts, and we built our business back, bigger and better than ever.

This is why I *love* "failure." I was fired for absolutely no reason, and most people would say I had a case to be upset, to say the least. When these things happen, I remind myself that my blood type is B-Positive and my last name is To-Risk. I don't look back. I say, "Next" and fail up!

Enough about me. Let's get down to business!

Up to this point I have told a few stories about the lessons I have learned. That's why I called the first half of this book "The Learning." I hope you can see that no matter where you stand in your life span, you realize that it is not where you come from that counts. What counts is where you want to go and actually doing something every day towards that goal. Remember TGIF? Not if you're not where you want to be Instead, use TGIS—The grind includes Saturday and Sunday!

For the second half of the book, I will illustrate how I took what I have learned and applied it to my various businesses or positions. I am calling it the "The Teaching," as it is my hope you will be able to broaden your view of what it takes to succeed in business.

By the way, at the end of each chapter from now on I will list the best resources I have read or heard about that taught me or inspired me about that chapter (or element, as I call them). So, keep your eyes open for these. May you find the nuggets that will serve you well and, better yet, allow you to serve others.

I will start with attitude and prospective:

The best books I have read on mindset are:

Can't Hurt Me by David Goggins
Rich Dad Poor Dad by Robert Kiyosaki

Part Two: The Teaching

Chapter 9: Business Elements

This part of the book is not written as a replacement for education nor do I claim to be an authority on all things business. However, I do know what you do not know about certain elements, which will hurt you and potentially kill your business. Likewise, what you do not demonstrate you know about business may be holding you back from those promotions! If you are not intimate with the way each principal part of a business runs, then you will always be making blind decisions, decisions that affect all of the other elements of the business. Having a grasp on the whole operation allows you to make strategic decisions that will set up the other departments for success! Talk about having *massive value*!

These next chapters are items I call business elements and are a compilation of what I have learned through years of working with some of the best mentors available, reading a ton of books, and making even more mistakes than I can remember. All of these elements are instrumental in the success of any business. You do not have to master every element of this book; however, you will absolutely need to be aware that every single element will impact your bottom line. Whether you hire people to help you with the elements you do not understand or do not enjoy doing, or you bite the bullet and go out and learn the things you need to know to be good at those elements until you can afford to hire people, you need to acknowledge they exist and every single element works in concert with the others to make a business successful.

The hardest part about writing this book is that I learn something new about how to do things better *every day*! So, how can I ever release this book when every day I learn something so useful to the person reading it? The answer is that this book is not meant for you to use as an instructional guide to run your business. It is meant for you to realize that there is *a lot* to understand, and there are so many resources to lean on, learn from, and utilize, so there is less chance of something blindsiding you and harpooning your efforts. With knowledge comes wisdom. Being wise means you retain the knowledge or the lessons of your experiences. It also means you know there are things you do not know. These chapters are a reference system to allow you to go and gain the knowledge in which you need to be aware. At the bottom of each chapter, I provided some resources I used.

So, what is business? Business is defined as "dealings or transactions, especially of an economic nature."

Since the first caveman traded a bird he hunted for some fur he needed, people treated the act as a transaction. They only contacted the fur man when they needed another pelt. To this day, this is how most people treat their service providers and how business owners treat their customers. They reach out to people they have not served and puke all over them with all the great things they can offer or sell to them without ever knowing anything personal about them or forging any kind of relationship.

At the end of the day, businesses need customers. It costs money to get customers through your system. That investment is referred to as the cost of acquisition. This is generally associated with the marketing element, which we will cover later, but it is part of the overall investment it takes to run your business. That ROI (return on investment) is what has historically been used to measure the success of a business by comparing the money left over for the owner (profits) versus the amount of money spent on making revenue, expenses, and overhead items.

The number one rule of new business: forget about ROI! It is the ROR (return on relationships) that gets you where you need to be. There has *never* been a time when connecting and forging real relationships has been easier or more accessible, no matter your situation.

There is one fundamental law that has proven to dictate sustainable success versus inevitable failure. It is an action that, if followed over time, you will find has an inverse proportionate value that directly correlates with the types of relationships you build with people. That is to say, you get what you give!

Start *now* by being a vessel of servitude. Treat everyone in your life who deserves your time (covered later) with the intention of helping them with their needs, or be the means to their end, but not as a transaction. Touch them, meaning stay in contact with them, but not on an annoying level. A text now and then, a handwritten letter, a mention on social media (how to use that for business later) is enough to keep you "top of mind" so when they need something from your business, or they know someone who will need something from your business, they think of you! If you treat enough people this way, you will never "look for business" in your life.

Best books I have read on building relationships/general business are:

Confessions of a Serial Salesman by Steve Nudelberg
Extreme Ownership by Jocko Willink and Leif Babin
Never Split the Difference by Chris Voss

Chapter 10: Wastin' Away in Operatorsville

Winston Churchill said, "If you are not a Liberal when you are young, you have no heart, and if you are not a Conservative when old, you have no brain."

I feel many of our working lives end up evolving like many of our life views.

When we start out, we have a sense of duty to please our boss and work as hard as we can to get some recognition in the form of praise, raises, or promotions.

As we gain experience over the years, we see it is not always the hours of hard work you put in or all of the effort you've dedicated to the company that gets rewarded. Sometimes bad leadership has you feeling like there are no opportunities to grow. Sometimes it is a failure to self-assess and admit that you are not seeking the correct avenues to advance your career. Sometimes it is political, nepotism, or perhaps there are other factors involved that are not being shared with you, but it is easy to become jaded or complacent with the uncertainty of the future.

It is generally at this point some of us start thinking, "I wouldn't treat people this way if I were the boss or if I owned this company." Your focus shifts from trying to impress others to "Why haven't those people I have worked so hard for all of these years recognized my value? Why am I working for them when I could do this myself, and 10 times better? *If only!*"

Then the *if only's* come next.

If only I had the money it would take to start my own company…

If only I had the time to put into starting small while I still worked here…

If only I had the silver spoon they clearly had when they started out…

There are a million reasons we create to justify not taking that risk of jumping ship and going at it on our own! And all these reasons have some merit to them. It is a *humongous risk* to start a small business! Entrepreneurship is not for the faint of heart! But there is something you can do that can prepare you for this. It is called intrapreneurship. The term "intrapreneurship" refers to a system that allows an employee to act like an entrepreneur within an organization and, more importantly, within the *safety* and *security* of the organization. Essentially, you are playing with house money!

If you want to begin your own business, start acting *as if!* Make decisions as if you own the company. Track your time, efficiency, and progress as if your decisions impact your paycheck. We will get into all of the elements of a business in later chapters, but start looking at your role in the company as a position you would hire someone for, and see if you would want them doing the things you are doing during your day.

If your organization is too small, take a few years to work for a larger organization. As I stated earlier, I went from a mom-and-pop contracting firm to working for the largest cable company in America. It was from this exposure I learned the core elements of business.

Sometimes factors in life call for a decision. And sometimes, that decision is to go for it! To buy a sign that says *Open For Business* and start the first day of the rest of your life as a small business owner! Because we have crafted our skills to the point of "mastery" and we think if we just do the right things for ourselves, there is no way we could fail! And sometimes, a fish jumps out of its bowl and lands on the counter only to realize he never noticed the water he lived in and the purpose it provided. And then you think, "Holy shit! What did I do?"

It is usually about six or seven months into the endeavor where we have built up some clientele by undercutting the competition. Clearly, you don't have the overhead and expenses of an established company, and there will be plenty of time to raise your prices once you get a following or some references from these clients.

Little by little, you get your pricing where you can turn a profit and acquire some important items such as insurance or an LLC. You do some branding and reinvest in a marketing plan. And before you know it, you have made that magical benchmark—the one-year goal!

You are so happy that you take a break from your 15-hour workdays and realize you haven't had a full day off in almost 8 months!

Then tax time rolls around. While you are pulling your numbers together for your taxes, you realize that you actually owe $18,000 to Uncle Sam, and you just spent an entire year to earn 50% less than you did as an employee. And worse, you don't know how you can possibly work any harder than you just have for a year straight to turn the tide.

All you have at your disposal is to raise your prices, but you do not have any of the resources to offer the client as justification for the rate increase, because you can't afford the staff to actually pull off what needs to be done. In addition, you are going after your next client by building a pipeline for your business or even balancing your books! Sure, your revenues are impressive, but your cash flow is nonexistent, and your balance sheet looks like a seesaw with an 800-pound gorilla on one side and a little girl on the other!

You've probably never even heard of the terms cash flow, balance sheet, and income statements.

This is the point where you have officially excelled at creating your own dead-end job, because when you stop working to do anything else to better your company, your income also takes the day off. Your work efforts are directly related to your income potential.

You borrow some money and start interviewing for your first hire, a protégé you can groom to replace you in the field who will free you up to do all of the other things necessary to grow your business.

Great idea! You are starting to get it, but there is a problem. It took you *years* to get as good as you got, and you charged a lot of money to come to work every day to perform the skills you cultivated through blood, sweat, and tears. And it's simply not in the budget to hire someone of your caliber to perform the functions needed to deliver the goods to the clients.

So, you start fresh with a newbie, and you figure you will be a better teacher to him than you had, because you have more incentive to get this trainee from beginner to expert. And the next reality sets in. They do not care as much as you do about the job, the client, or having this opportunity as a springboard to a rewarding trade.

To them, it is 9 to 5, and half the time they don't even take notes when you show them what to do.

They don't sweat the small stuff, and there are inconsistencies with the quality of their work. And worse, when it comes to crunch time, they have plans to go to the skate park with their cousin or something important like that. You're often left seething and thinking, "It wouldn't even *be* crunch time if I weren't taking it so slow by watching them muddle through tasks I could do in 1/10th of the time! So, why am I paying someone to make my life harder?"

You begin the cycle of either letting them go or dealing with them not bothering to show up after a few weeks. You lather, rinse, and repeat with these newbies.

This is surely beginning to turn into the definition of insanity—repeating the same actions over and over but expecting different results.

Welcome to *operatorsville*! How you got here you haven't a clue!

Lessons Learned:

1. Nobody will care for your business or have as much passion about it as you will.

2. If you are a true operator, nobody will match your level of quality.

3. If you spend all of your time working *in* your business, you will never learn how to work *on* your business.

Learning Curve:

1. You will need a process for hiring someone with the aptitude for learning the skills needed to replace you.

2. In the meantime, you may hire someone to do the things you are not good at, such as:

- A bookkeeper who can manage the expenditures and income

- A marketer who can advertise or at least do some social media posts to help build your brand

- A salesperson who can keep your pipeline filled

- A virtual CEO who can create and review a business plan with you at least quarterly

- A virtual CFO who can review your balance sheets, cash flow statements, and income statements monthly with you so you can have optics on your financial health

Best books I have read on building employees are:

Leaders Made Here by Mark Miller
The Dichotomy of Leadership by Jocko Willink and Leif Babin

Chapter 11: Human Resources Elements

Along with the other elements in this book, the HR (human resources) element is a crucial and often overlooked part of your business. As with anything in life, the resources will often have a direct correlation with your chances of having success. What is more valuable than the human resource? At some point, whether you are climbing a corporate ladder or opening a lemonade stand, if you are doing things the right way, you will need help from other people. This is where having the knowledge of what goes into finding the right people to surround yourself with and keeping them happy and challenged pays off *big time*. But this is much more difficult than most imagine.

From understanding where you can find the help you need, to figuring out the right mental and personality acuities that will match your company's culture, to having the hires actually stick and produce with as little turnover as possible, this all has double-digit effects on your profit margins. And when dealing with a start-up company or department, having the advantage of these elements can be the difference between success and failure!

Building your bench (having someone lined up to take the position of a person who is leaving) is also important in so many ways. It allows you to ensure your results do not take a nosedive when you lose a key point person. Having strong teams creates competition and breeds a learning culture, providing you create one.

Clearly, a small start-up business cannot support multiple levels for every position, but being aware that hiring the right people who are open to learning and willing to perform tasks other than those they were hired for ensures the team is successful because of the efforts of the group instead of the selfishness of the individual.

Knowing how to make people *feel* valued and set up for success is paramount. You must understand that getting the best out of every employee is a skill learned by the best leaders. Any "boss" can regurgitate stats and benchmarks, but true leaders mentor, shepherd, encourage, empower, ask questions, and teach their employees. Capture the hearts and minds of the employees, and they will go through walls for you in return.

Here are some HR elements you should be aware of, no matter what size your company is. These items will need attention and forethought.

Recruiting

- Interviewing
- Hiring
- Recommending
- Referring

Training and Development

- Evaluating
- Documenting
- Certifying

Compensation

- Evaluating
- Documenting
- Recording
- Tracking

Job Analysis/Job Design

- Evaluating
- Comparing
- Building Efficiencies

Performance Management

- Evaluating

- Coaching
- Celebrating
- Promoting/Firing

Labor Relations

- Rewarding
- Encouraging
- Mentioning
- Celebrating

Here is a glimpse of all the benefits employees will be expecting from a company competing with established companies:

- Insurance (Life)
- Insurance (Health PPO)
- Insurance (Health HMO)
- Insurance (Deductible)
- Insurance (Co-Payment)
- Insurance (Out of Pocket Max)
- Insurance (Prescription Coverage)
- Insurance (Dental)
- Insurance (Short-term)
- Insurance (Long-term)
- Insurance (Vehicle)

- Retirement Plans
- Pension Plans
- Investments
- Vacations
- Sick Leave
- Personal Time
- Short-term Disability
- Maternity Leave
- Bereavement Leave

You will need to overcome not being able to offer these benefits until you "make it," and you likely won't "make it" alone. You must offset the lack of benefits with *value, appreciation, pride, ownership equity, and progress.*

Best book I have read on HR is:

Developing Exemplary Performance One Person at a Time by Michael Sabbag

Chapter 12: Time Management Elements

What is the number one commodity in the world? It is not gold, nor silver, nor even bitcoin. It is time. Running a business for 10 years and then losing it for whatever reason hurts in many ways, but the time you lose is priceless. Even though you can start another venture and get back all of the gains, toys, and confidence you may lose, you will never get back the time.

Avoid all the starts and stops by using the lessons discussed in this book. Time has a way of doing a few mean tricks. One is moving much faster than we realize, and another is allowing us to create horrible habits.

We tend to procrastinate doing things we do not look forward to and pay attention to the easy and fast tasks, because we feel like we are accomplishing things. But quantity does not equal quality when it comes to managing your time.

One of the ways to keep the plates spinning is to know which plates to let fall. Learning the power of *no* is an amazing and underutilized skill. The following two tips have made a major impact on my ability to harness the *no* and review my choices and compare my actions to the progress or losses my company or departments have had during any given period of time.

Below are two really simple ways to make *huge* gains in your personal and business life!

Here are four questions for figuring out what deserves your time and energy:

1. Is it important and urgent? Do it. Do it now.

2. Is it important but not urgent? Schedule it. Schedule it now.

3. Is it urgent but not important? If possible, delegate it.

4. Is it not important and not urgent? Forget it!

Calendar it:

1. If it needs to get attention, it needs to be on your calendar.

2. Schedule things in 15-minute increments (minimum).

3. If it isn't on your calendar, it will not get done.

4. If you have multiple calendars, merge them.

5. Personal and professional plans and activities can be on the same calendar.

Best time management book I have read is:

The 80/20 Principle by Richard Koch

Chapter 13: The Element of Understanding Roles

So much emphasis these days is placed on your identity and being proud of who you are at your core, not what the world can see or the labels that others have placed on you over time. As discussed earlier in the book, your mindset will dictate your inner view and belief of what you are capable. Understanding your identity is crucial for the role you will have in any business setting. For any company to truly thrive and grow, it takes two main and very different characteristics.

One is the entrepreneurial spirit and mindset. The second, although equally important, is the managerial drive and discipline. Some people have both, but no one has enough time and energy to fill both roles for any extended period. Sooner or later, when you expand your company or department, you will need to understand your true strengths and surround yourself with the opposite.

Here are some key elements of each to look out for:

An entrepreneur creates the message for the company.

Descriptors:

- Provider
- Impatient
- Creative
- High thinkers
- Convincing
- Works well alone
- Communicator
- Risk-takers
- Passionate
- Visionary
- Relationship builders
- Short attention span
- Does not work well in groups
- Impulsive

A manager communicates the message of the owner.

Descriptors:

- Methodical
- Systematic
- Equalizer
- Patient
- Communicator
- Communicative

- Works well in groups
- Sense of urgency
- Process driven
- Decentralized
- Empathetic
- Service oriented/Pleaser
- Anal retentive
- Micromanagers
- Works well alone

Communication Tools:
- Face-to-face
- Telephone
- Skype/Zoom
- Email
- Texts
- Snail Mail

Meetings Types:
- Client
- Management
- Board
- Team/Staff
- Safety/Tailgate
- Leadership

The meetings should have an agenda which is pre-planned and distributed to the participants. The meeting should be interactive and review items such as:

- Production versus billing comparisons
- KPIs reviewed by market/project goals (forecast versus actual)
- Celebrate meeting and exceeding forecasts and sharing success stories
- Correction plans if shortfalls are happening
- Forecasts (adjust based on results)
- Cover selected company processes and best practices
- Equipment/personnel transfers
- Headcount needs/changes/plans
- Your agenda items (must be provided 24 hours before the meeting)

Meeting Cadence:

- Held weekly, scheduled for one hour but will last until we get to everyone
- All leaders must be present
- No distractions (cell phones off the table and preferably in a pocket)
- If joining remotely, video is preferred; plan ahead

- In truck/in field, connections permitting; dial-in if no video is possible
- Hold meetings more frequently if friction is leading to conflict or impacting the business
- Be accountable for your department's results and direction

Solving Issues:

- Choose top three topics impacting company
- Identify the *real* issue (one sentence, root of the problem)
- Move to discuss and stay on point until it is solved; no rants
- Everyone participates in the discussion
- Important to make a decision. When we cannot, the owner will rule
- Present a united front going forward
- It's okay to disagree, but everyone must buy in

Employee Problem Solving:

- Employees are not permitted to go around the leader
- The leader may "hear the employee out" but should refrain from making a decision
- After listening, the leader should ask the employee his thoughts for a solution to the issue
- Then the leader can discuss the ideas and suggest or implement a solution that best fits the issue

- If the solution conflicts with the delivery of expected deliverables or company policies, the owner must be involved before the solution is implemented

Information Items:

Plans	Goals/KPIs/WIGS
Forecasting	Lead indicators
Lag indicators	Scorecards
Policies	Changes
Projects	Initiatives
Innovations	Milestones
Successes	Roadblocks

The best book I have read about understanding roles is:

Rocket Fuel by Gino Wickman and Mark C. Winters

Chapter 14: Financial Elements

I have ADHD (attention deficit hyperactivity disorder), which makes reading fun. I have the same problem with reading as I do with speaking. It is like I am constantly playing *Name That Tune* but with words! I tend to *think* I know the point that person (or author) is heading towards with just the first few words.

This means I am usually thinking of a counterpoint or related story to respond with while the person is still mid-sentence. Or if I am reading, I will literally take the words in a sentence and jumble the letters to make entirely different words to create my narrative in order to support my presuppositional thoughts. I call it dyslexia, but it isn't that I jumble the letters so I can't read; it is that I rearrange the letters to make up new words. Most of the time I am *totally* off-base. The old saying "You have two ears and one mouth. Use them proportionally" rings true. For reading, I say I have two eyes and one mind. Use them proportionally.

It is this reason that a lifelong goal of mine is to A) be a better listener and B) be a better reader. That is, to learn how to be an *active listener* and a *purposeful reader*, to take in what I am hearing (or reading) as it comes and allow the story to unfold in the storyteller's own way and time. Often, people have told the story over and over and have rehearsed the speech in their own way, and when you cut them off, you are interrupting their routine, and they mentally vapor lock, so what you are responding with is actually not being processed. When you listen to their story actively—nodding, mirroring their expressions and voice inflections with a quip or a "Get out!"—you separate yourself from most people, and the speaker will tend to feel heard and value your conversation more.

Likewise, a person may be giving you excuses or reasons for falling short of a goal or a deliverable. Often, while affording them the time to talk, they will be giving you clues for your counterargument, or you will simply hear enough to figure out they are full of shit. Either way, you can shorten those conversations by letting them run out of gas.

As far as reading, I have gone down many rabbit holes to learn how to read with more comprehension. As you probably know, your mind can process data hundreds of times faster than you can process it cognitively. So, if you practice reading enough, there is a point where you will stop hearing the voice in your head, and you will visualize a movie in your mind by seeing the words. You literally see a movie of your own creation based on the words you are reading.

Of course, this takes a lot of reading, and there are a lot of tricks, which most people call speedreading, you must learn to get there. For example, not moving your eyeballs, cutting off the first and last inch of words at the margins (because your mind will fill in those missing words), and using a ruler or guide to control your descent down the page.

Personally, I have learned to lean into my tendencies, acknowledge them, and skim a book two or three times periodically to grab the nuggets I want. Then, I leave the rest for another sitting. If something grabs my attention, I can generally read more purposefully, because it has relevance to an upcoming situation or I have just gone through something I can relate to it.

The reason I am telling you this about myself during the finance elements part of the book is because listening to your counterparts is vital to understanding their story. And believe it or not, your business is trying to tell you a story.

Warren Buffett has described accounting as "the language of business." What a statement that is! If you can master reading the numbers, you will be able to see what your business is telling you. It will give you have clarity and optics about what is happening in your business. This will allow you to make changes before the credits are rolling.

The best explanation I ever received regarding this subject and these three items was by a man named Keith Cunningham. Keith is a speaker I have seen at two business mastery seminars, on two continents, which Tony Robbins hosted. Keith has taught critical business skills, mentored and coached thousands of top executives and entrepreneurs around the world.

Keith teaches us that we need to compare our business to a sporting event. There are certain numbers we look for to see if our team is winning or losing at any given time. There are stats that tell you about the activities of the game, how the team is performing. These activities can convert to numbers, but sometimes, even though the stats can indicate a winning game, in reality your team can still be losing on the scoreboard. That is why you need to know how to convert the numbers into words. That is the story of your business.

The whole point of a business is to acquire assets. Assets lead to sales, and sales lead to profits, which the business owner converts into *cash*. This is a business in its simplest form. There are three different kinds of cash. Two types of cash are financing cash and investing cash, but operating cash is the best type of cash there is!

Keith provides the tools and strategies used by the pros to not only make money but also keep it! A self-made millionaire, Keith is an expert at helping business owners turn fledgling businesses into highly profitable companies with explosive growth. I will not need a spoiler alert for Keith's great content, because no one can deliver it like he can, but here are the "CliffsNotes" to reading the three most important "dials" of accounting to know where you stand in your business.

Like most great stories, the financial story is told in three acts, and it is up to you whether it will be a fairytale or a horror flick! It is not telling you verbally, nor is it telling you its story with the written word. It is telling you its story with numbers.

The three acts are like the Holy Trinity of accounting:

- Balance sheets
- Income statements
- Cash flow statements

The balance sheet:

The balance sheet is a list of "things and stuff" which are listed on a page in accordance with whether we own them (assets) or owe on them (liabilities).

Every financial transaction we make in our business impacts this scorecard.

The balance sheet is a snapshot of your business at any given time. Every balance sheet will start with "As of."

This is a world atlas showing you what your company has or owes. Your assets will always equal your earnings in the income statement when run at the same time.

The income statement:

The income statement is sometimes also called a statement of operations or profit and loss statement (P&L). The income statement shows profit, which is a *theory*. You cannot spend profits! It is designed to tell you if your revenue is exceeding your expenses. That is it! This is a movie covering a period of time. It has a beginning and an end, usually a month, a quarter, or a year.

- The top part shows the revenue, or sales or income.
- The second part lists the expenses.
- What you are left with are the profits, or earnings, or the net income.

When most people get this statement quarterly or, even worse, yearly, they tend to look at the figures at the bottom; hence, the term "bottom line."

If this number on the bottom line is a good number, you will go and have a drink! And if it's a bad number, you will go and have a drink! This is a street map showing where your earnings came from or went.

Cash flow statement:

This is a worksheet showing you where your cash is coming from or going. The cash flow statement is also a movie. It is a living document which will show you the position of your company over a period of time. There are three parts to a cash flow statement:

- Operating cash

- Investments

- Financing

Each section will have positive (owned) and negative (owed) numbers. The total of the positives minus the negatives will total the amount of *cash* you have access to in your company. This is a *real thing* you can spend, provided it is a positive number.

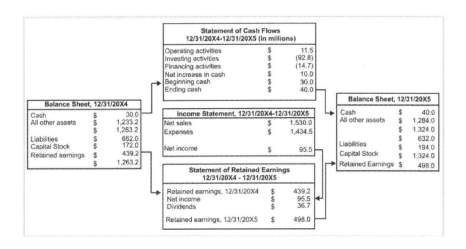

The best books I have read about business finance are:

The Ultimate Blueprint for an Instantly Successful Business by Keith Cunningham

Keys To The Vault by Keith Cunningham

Chapter 15: Contract Elements

The important thing to keep in mind when dealing with contracts is that interpretation is your enemy. Whether you are writing a contract or receiving one, the terms and words are all there for a reason, and they can and will be used against you in a court of law.

There is no such thing as "the spirit" of a contract, although I have heard that phrase several times. They have never held up under scrutiny. It is important to open your mind and think as if you are the other party, only without scruples or a conscience. A contract is the letter of the law and will be referred to at every impasse or disagreement of the relationship.

Try to be as specific as possible, and when in doubt of a legal term, look it up or ask for the help of an attorney. I find that most attorneys will want to change things or add things just to prove they were needed or show how smart they are. So, resist accepting everything the legal eagles return at face value. After all, their job is to protect you, not to assure you that both parties can operate and be successful. There is such a thing as a win-win situation, and a properly written contract is the first step toward that scenario.

I have been involved in more than a few projects which have been bitten by the terms of a contract, and it has cost my firm hundreds of thousands of dollars. Conversely, I was involved in one that literally saved my firm over two million dollars.

Remember that any deal agreed to verbally *is not worth the paper it isn't written on.*

Here are some elements of a contract you should look up and have a cursory understanding of before committing to a binding contract:

Information Items:

Describing
Specifying
Scheduling
Defining
Conditioning
Localities
Safety
3rd Parties
Rights
Termination
Minimums
Equipment
Uniforms
Waivers
Harmony
Counterparts
Qualifiers
Bonds
Publicity
Fees
Guarantees
Renewals
Attachments
Executions

Liens
Itemizing
Dead lining
Explaining
Provisioning
Concessions
Quality
Extensions
Changes
Claims
Thresholds
Transportation
Logos
Personnel
Licenses
Considerations
Regulations
Confidentiality
Communications
Certifying
Terms
Principles
Addendums

Clarifying
Addressing
Inspecting
Testing
Governing
Permitting
Defaults
Notices
Moderating
Insurance
Material
Cleanliness
IDs
Affiliations
Certificates
Registrations
Indemnifying
Non-Disclosures
Taxes
Payments
Retainage
Acceptance
Revisions

No book suggestions, only personal experience. Sorry!

Chapter 16: Sales Elements

When it comes to covering sales in a book like this, where we touch a little on a lot of business aspects, it is tough to provide advice which will help every reader. The range of what people can sell, who they can sell to, how they communicate with potential clients, and what regulations are in place for the sale can impact the strategy or advice one can provide.

But with that said…

There are several universal principles involved with selling that can be applied to most selling situations. I will touch on some of these universal tips and principles which have served me well over the years in various sales applications, but they are in no particular order.

Tip # 1

Never be in the position to *sell* anything. You want to be the person who people think of when they have a problem that needs a solution. When people know, like, and trust you, you will never *sell* anything again.

Selling should be synonymous with helping or educating. After all, the word "sales" is derived from a Scandinavian phrase which means "to serve."

Tip # 2

You must believe in and have *intimate knowledge* of the product or service you are offering or providing. If you are involved with a substandard product or you do not have the proper understanding of the need the product or service fills, how are you ever going to convey to the prospect that this is their answer?

Tip # 3

Be the thought leader in the space. When you offer to give your knowledge and experience to those newer in your industry, you will end up learning more about people and see new perspectives that will help sharpen your skills, give you more empathy, and provide new experiences to share with your clients. It comes full circle!

Tip # 4

When your prospective client asks you a question about your product or service, do not automatically start regurgitating a list of how it does this or that. Instead, try answering, "Yes, but *why*? What makes you ask that question?" There is a greater wealth of information awaiting you there. Ask why that is important to them. With the answers from them regarding their concerns, you can pinpoint the real need they have.

Tip # 5

Grow elephant skin! You will be told *no* and rejected repeatedly…if you are doing it right, that is. There are a million examples of successful people who were rejected countless times before working out their processes to overcome the *no's* and start getting enough *yes's* to pay the rent.

Colonel Sanders, the founder of Kentucky Fried Chicken, has a very famous story illustrating the power of persistence. A lot of people know about the KFC secret recipe story, where he started his business after retiring penniless and on Social Security at 65 years of age.

Colonel Sanders traveled door-to-door to houses and restaurants all over his local area. He wanted to partner with someone to help promote his chicken recipe. He was met with little enthusiasm. He started traveling by car to numerous restaurants and cooked his fried chicken on the spot for the owners. If the owner liked the chicken, they would enter into a handshake agreement to sell the Colonel's chicken. Legend has it that Colonel Sanders heard 1,009 *no's* before he heard his first *yes*.

Okay, let me repeat that. He was turned down one thousand nine times before his proposition was accepted once! That *yes* was a nickel for each piece of chicken the restaurant sold. The restaurant would receive packets of the Colonel's secret herbs and spices to keep them from learning the recipe. Today there are 6,000 franchises selling his trademark chicken.

What a lot of people do not know is that he had very little success throughout his life. It isn't like he was blessed with the taste of success and knew that sticking to his plan would pay off because he had done it a time or two before.

Sanders was born in 1890. At the age of six, his father died, leaving him to take care of his family. In the seventh grade, he dropped out of school and left home to go work as a farmhand. At 16, he faked his age to enlist in the United

States Army. After the Army, he got hired by the railway as a laborer until he got fired for fighting with a coworker.

While he worked for the railway, he studied law until he ruined his legal career by getting into another fight. Sanders had to move back in with his mother and get a job selling life insurance, then managed to get himself fired for insubordination.

In 1920 he founded a ferry boat company. Later, he tried cashing in his ferry boat business to create a lamp manufacturing company but discovered another company already sold a better version of his lamp.

At the age of 40 he began selling chicken and washing dishes in a service station. As he began to advertise his food, an argument with a competitor resulted in a deadly shootout, which left an associate of the Colonel's dead and Harland Sanders on trial. He was acquitted, and four years later he bought a motel which burned to the ground along with his restaurant. However, this determined man rebuilt and operated a new motel until World War II forced him to close it down.

After all this failure, he retired at 65 years of age. When he received his Social Security check for $105, he contemplated suicide. He sat under a tree and wrote down what he thought he was capable of accomplishing. He decided that of all his life's vocations, frying chicken was the one thing he could do better than anyone else. So, he got up, borrowed $87 against his next Social Security check, and bought some chicken to sell door-to-door in his Kentucky neighborhood.

You know the rest of the story. But tell me, if your soul was worn down to the point of contemplating suicide, how many *no's* would you have experienced before saying, "Okay, that's it"?

10 *no's?* 25 *no's?* 50 *no's?* 100 *no's?* 200 *no's?* 500 *no's?* How about 800 *no's?*

For sure, at 1,000 *no's* you know you would have said, "Golf it is."

But he finally got a *yes* at 1,010 pitches.

How much did Colonel Sanders believe in his product? I would say he had an unwavering belief.

Tip # 6

There are a lot of other nuances regarding the sales process that need to be tailored to the specifics of your target market. Things like:

- Having your pitch down pat. (Hint: It should not sound like a pitch.)
- Role-play to be comfortable with different scenarios
- If it is a larger purchase, having both parties present for the pitch
- Pre-qualifying your client(s)
- Illustrating the benefits and advantages of your product or service
- Starting with the Big Mac
- The art of the add-ons
- Total transparency versus smoke and mirrors
- The River Technique (Zig Ziglar)
- Asking the right questions
- Storytelling
- Creating a *yes* pattern
- Creating a need and filling it
- Handling objections
- Asking for objections

Closing techniques:

- ABC

- Assuming the close
- He who talks first loses
- Asking for the check
- Handing a pen to the client for a signature
- Parking in a "sold" spot after a test drive
- Avoiding setting your own financial limits in your head
- Reverse psychology: taking the deal off the table
- Selling on a return policy (*weak*)

Best books I have read on sales are:

Thinking Fast and Slow by Daniel Kahneman

Secrets of Closing the Sale by Zig Ziglar

Go For No! by Richard Fenton and Andrea Waltz

Chapter 17: Marketing Elements

No market, no sales. Know marketing, know sales. It is that simple. It has been said that marketing controls the budgets. It is the intellectual and creative force of the business. Capturing the attention and loyalty of the public is the goal. There are so many books written on this topic alone that I will not claim to be able to tell you one thing that has not already been revealed. But I will warn you of a few mistakes that most make in this element that can mean the difference between failure and success.

The first thing that most businesses do is think of an item, product, service, or platform *they* think the public would want. Then they do a ton of research and development building towards a launch. They follow that up with the marketing. They make a list of the great features and benefits of their wares. Finally, they let the public know how this product or service will fill the void in everyone's lives and ask, "Want to buy it?"

It has been discovered by watching the *giants* like Nike, Apple, and AT&T that the mousetrap is built backwards. They have proven that the reverse process is the most effective method to touch people in a way that creates raving lifelong fans (short for fanatics). This is the whole point, isn't it?

Do you want customers to buy something from you, or do you want clients who will stand in line for hours before your product becomes available?

These guys start with *why* people do things. And then they build the item, product, service, or platform to fill the need in those specific people's lives. They ask, "Aren't you tired of having this void in your life? Don't you wish you felt in control? Wouldn't you like to be connected like this? Well, here is just the item that will allow you to have that. Want to buy it?" They start by connecting with the *why* and then move to the *what*.

Half of these companies' commercials do not even feature the product or service they are selling. They only describe the *feeling* you will get from associating with the brand. That is marketing genius.

The second part of marketing is tracking performance and ultimately looking at the ROI. That is the revenue made versus the cost of the advertisement. There are a lot of marketing options these days. There are also a lot of ways to measure the ROI. Adaptability and testing are key for finding the sweet spot.

I believe that sincerity and honesty prevail. Attracting clients to make contact is the win if you can offer an honest, amazing, over-the-top customer service experience! Most people would rather give their business to a company they can call with a problem and have an empathetic ear on the other end who, number one, affirms there is a problem, and, number two, will do everything possible to resolve the problem. That creates loyalty and raving lifelong fans!

These are the people who create the most coveted marketing there is: the personal introduction! Even more precious than a referral is the introduction. When someone brings a person to your company and personally vouches for what sets you apart from the competition, your chances of doing meaningful business with that person are through the roof!

I have been in more than a few boardrooms for marketing planning sessions, and I have seen a lot of stuff thrown against a whiteboard. But if you can figure out the *why* for your *what*, then the *who's* will line up for you.

The best resource to explain this is an old TED Talk by Simon Sinek called "How Great Leaders Inspire Action." I know, it doesn't sound like a marketing related video, but it is.

Chapter 18: The Last Bite of The Elephant

To wrap up this book (a sentence I never envisioned myself typing), I would like to summarize by offering the advice I follow when I need to change anything in my life.

Show up. Ninety percent of doing is in the start.

As one of my childhood idols, Don Shula, used to say, "It's the start that stops most people." This is so important that I had to say it again. Joe Rogan often talks about the power of showing up. Even when you are not sure how to start something, just make up your mind to act. Nobody starts off with greatness. It is only achieved by practicing perfectly.

Get to the root of your *why*.

People will say that your *why* is in your heart, or your gut, or your soul. It is actually in the limbic part of your brain. This is the part that is responsible for feeling, intuition, and purpose. You need to use the neocortex part, which is responsible for logic and communication, to connect the words that really capture the feeling and purpose for *why* you want to change your life. This is the only way that will keep you trying when, not if, you meet resistance and failures on your journey.

Do not be afraid of failing.

Some of my biggest failures, *devastating failures*, have led to relationships I never would have had otherwise. That includes being in the position I was in when I met my wife. In 2009 I experienced my biggest failure when the housing bubble burst, and I was forced to shut down my company. I had to ultimately claim bankruptcy and take a J.O.B. purely for the health insurance to cover my boys, and that's what led to us meeting.

Brand yourself.

Times change. Fads come and go. People who think they need something today will not even remember that thing five years from now. Who will still be there? *You.* You need to be what people remember when they need the next big thing, or advice, or an introduction, or to be inspired or motivated. You will be relevant and in demand if you brand yourself and make real connections with people, which leads me to…

Make real connections.

ROR = Return on Relationships. This is the closest thing to a secret to success. Real, true, caring, and selfless relationships. Build them high and wide. This is the only commodity that will stand the test of time. Your currency in life is your name.

Stay hungry.

Your *why* will change over time. You will hit a plateau. It is not natural to have an ascending timeline of success. There are peaks and valleys, but eventually you will be on solid ground with tons of wins under your belt, and the fight you started will not seem fulfilling. It is okay to re-examine your *why* and change your direction if *you change you*. You will need to challenge yourself in many ways. Money cannot be the motivator. It must be the passion you seek, or you will lose momentum.

The power of increments.

Always envision your future self and work every day towards becoming that person, just 1% at a time. Even if that means two steps forward and one step back. Do not give up, and take the next step.

The college option.

I believe that everyone is different, and college is not for everyone, but learning is. College can be used to gain a great foundation in writing, math, speaking, and commitment. It is also a great place to learn how to learn, especially night classes, as it is usually filled with adults who genuinely want to better their lives and are there to learn. A degree should not be the goal; picking up the skills is the goal.

Here is a beautiful post I saw on a blog, which encapsulates everything I have written about in this book with elegance and simplicity. Written by Ruben Chavez, it is called "Think. Grow. Prosper."

Habits to Help You Prosper:

Network

Dream Big

Plan Ahead

Get Up Early

Stay Focused

Watch Less TV

Invest In Yourself

Read More Books

Avoid Time Wasters

Take Calculated Risks

Write Down Your Goals

Live On Less Than You Make

Make Your Health A Priority

Do Work That Matters To You

Learn From People You Admire

Foster Meaningful Relationships

Cultivate An Attitude Of Gratitude

Take Action, Especially When It's Scary

Have A Powerful And Inspiring "WHY"

Life is short, my friends. Go *pro*.

Why did you turn to this page? Wasn't the last page a *great ending?* This must mean that you are looking for a way to *go pro*. We can help with that, my friend. You can reach me at www.jeremytorisk.com.

I would love to hear from you and see if I can offer any knowledge or services to enrich your life, help you reach a goal, or simply connect to create a lasting relationship!

When I started this book, it was to get some old feelings off my chest and get them onto paper during the COVID-19 lockdown of 2020. But through chance introductory and virtual meetings of some amazing people, namely the Nudelberg family at On the Ball Ventures and everyone in their ever-growing network of unbelievable givers, I totally changed the intention of this exercise and decided to share my stories, failures, and successes with you. I hope I have touched you in some way.

Remember, follow your passion, and do not listen to those who try to stop you from dreaming. Call on me if you ever need a helping hand or just an ear to listen to you.

Thank you,

JT

Made in the USA
Columbia, SC
13 September 2021

44841609R00080